SPECTRUM®

Test Practice 3

With Free Online Resources for each U.S. State

Published by Spectrum®
An imprint of Carson-Dellosa Publishing LLC
Greensboro, NC

Spectrum®
An imprint of Carson-Dellosa Publishing LLC
P.O. Box 35665
Greensboro, NC 27425 USA

Printed in the U.S.A. • All rights reserved.   ISBN: 978-1-62057-595-6

01-002137784

The Common Core State Standards

What Are the Standards?

The Common Core State Standards have been adopted by most U.S. states. They were developed by a state-led initiative to make sure all students are prepared for success in college and in the global, twenty-first century workforce. They provide a clear understanding of what students are expected to learn in English language arts and mathematics.

These new learning standards for your child are:

- Rigorous.

- Based on the best available evidence and research.

- Aligned with college and work expectations.

- Benchmarked to the highest educational standards from around the world.

What Do the English Language Arts Standards Mean for My Student?

In grade 3, English language arts standards focus on reading, writing, speaking and listening, and language skills (grammar and usage).

These standards set expectations for what it means to be a skilled reader and writer in the twenty-first century. They provide strategies for reading fiction and nonfiction closely and attentively. They help students look for evidence and make critical judgments about the vast amount of print and digital information available.

What Do the Mathematics Standards Mean for My Student?

Examples of grade 3 mathematics standards include operations and algebraic thinking (multiplying and dividing within 100) and fractions (understanding fractions such as $\frac{1}{4}$, $\frac{1}{3}$, $\frac{1}{2}$).

These standards increase the depth and focus of math topics studied in each grade. Instead of sampling a wide variety of skills each year, students work to develop deep understanding and mastery of a few concepts.

Free Online State-Specific Test Practice

For additional **free** *Spectrum Test Practice* resources customized to your child's grade level and the U.S. state where you live, follow these instructions:

1. Go to:

   carsondellosa.com/spectrum

2. Click on *Spectrum Test Practice Free Online Materials* and register to download your free practice pages.

3. Download and print PDF pages customized for your state and your child's grade level.

Online Features Include:

- Links to Common Core State Standards information for your state

- A comprehensive practice test aligned to Common Core English language arts and mathematics standards for your child's grade level

- State-specific test items within the practice test, designated by this symbol: **1.**

  These items are aligned to the unique standards that have been adopted by your state in addition to Common Core State Standards.

- An answer key for practice test pages

How to Use This Book

Time spent practicing for standardized tests will benefit your child greatly. With the adoption of Common Core State Standards by most U.S. states, educators are relying more than ever on test results to compare your child's progress with that of others around the nation and the world. The resources in this book will help ease anxieties and prepare your child for test day.

What's Inside?

- **Lesson pages** contain sample questions and examples related to a specific skill. The assumption is that your student has received prior instruction on the topics. These pages can provide focused practice.

- **Sample tests** are shorter tests with questions about one subtopic.

- **Practice tests** are comprehensive tests with questions about the entire content area.

Practice Options

Choose how you will use the materials to meet the needs of your student.

- Select pages matching the skills your student needs to practice most.

- Assign lesson pages for practice throughout the week. End the week with a sample or practice test related to those skills.

- Administer a timed practice test in a quiet setting. For a third grade student, allow 1.25 minutes per question. After the test, check answers together and talk about what was most difficult.

Test-Taking  Clues

- Look for the symbol shown above throughout the book. Talk about the clues with your child.

- Read and review directions and examples. Talk about how test questions look and point out words and phrases that often appear in directions.

- Skip difficult questions, returning to them if time allows.

- Guess at questions you do not know.

- Answer all the questions.

- Try to stay relaxed and approach the test with confidence!

READING: VOCABULARY

● **Lesson 1: Synonyms**

Directions: Read each item. Choose the answer that means the same or about the same as the underlined word.

Examples

A. **delicious pie**
- (A) salty
- (B) bad
- (C) gentle
- (D) tasty ●

B. **She picked a meadow flower.**
- (F) iceberg
- (G) swamp
- (H) field ●
- (J) forest

Clue If you are not sure about the right answer, say the phrase once using each answer choice to replace the underlined word.

● **Practice**

1. **automobile show**
- (A) train
- (B) car ●
- (C) plane
- (D) wagon

2. **faint cry**
- (F) soft ●
- (G) loud
- (H) sad
- (J) angry

3. **ordinary day**
- (A) strange
- (B) memorable
- (C) rainy
- (D) usual ●

4. **The castle flew a bright banner.**
- (F) cloud
- (G) flag ●
- (H) balloon
- (J) talk

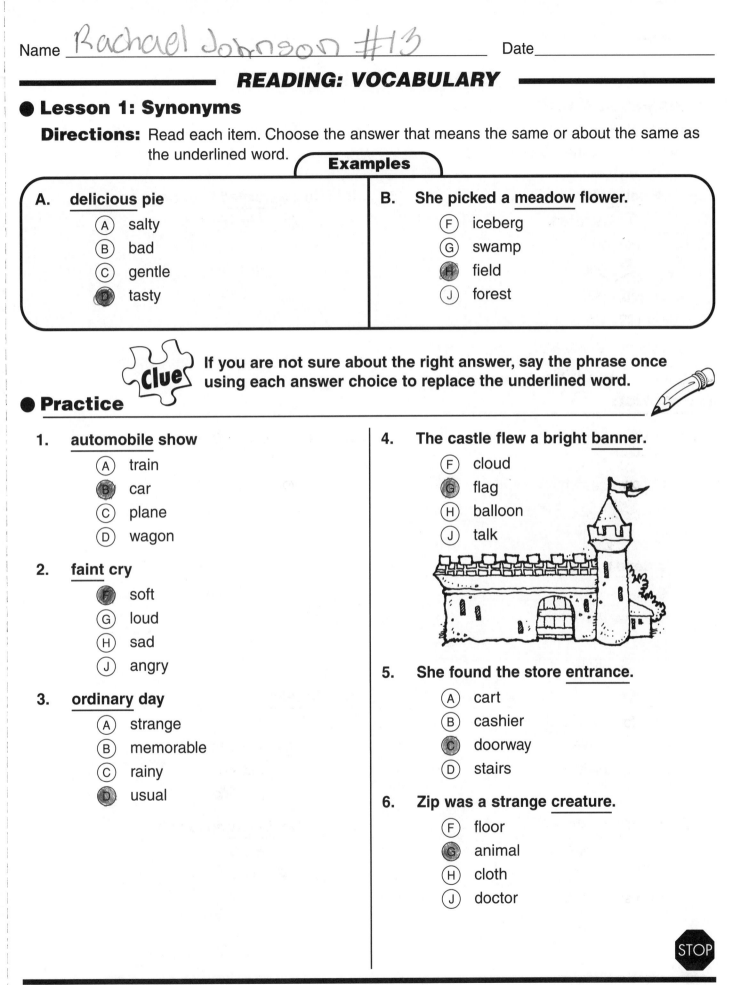

5. **She found the store entrance.**
- (A) cart
- (B) cashier
- (C) doorway ●
- (D) stairs

6. **Zip was a strange creature.**
- (F) floor
- (G) animal ●
- (H) cloth
- (J) doctor

STOP

READING: VOCABULARY

● Lesson 2: Vocabulary Skills

Directions: Read each item. Choose the answer that means the same or about the same as the underlined word.

Examples

A. **A pair of birds**
- (A) a dozen
- (B) white
- (C) one
- (D) two

B. **To be worried is to be—**
- (F) friendly
- (G) concerned
- (H) lost
- (J) injured

Clue Your first answer choice is probably correct. Don't change it unless you are sure another answer is better.

● Practice

1. **A secret bond**
- (A) tie
- (B) search
- (C) trap
- (D) light

2. **Attend a class**
- (F) skip
- (G) pass
- (H) like
- (J) go to

3. **A prize pig**
- (A) award-winning
- (B) clever
- (C) pink
- (D) bad

4. **Towering cliff**
- (F) tipping over
- (G) handmade
- (H) high
- (J) low

5. **To shoplift is to—**
- (A) buy
- (B) steal
- (C) weigh
- (D) walk

6. **A basement is like a—**
- (F) staircase
- (G) attic
- (H) kitchen
- (J) cellar

7. **To faint is to—**
- (A) bow
- (B) wake up
- (C) pass out
- (D) pretend

8. **To be disturbed is to be—**
- (F) noisy
- (G) calm
- (H) joyful
- (J) upset

STOP

READING: VOCABULARY

● **Lesson 3: Antonyms**

Directions: Read each item. Choose the answer that means the opposite of the underlined word.

Examples

A.   **The ladder is unsafe.**

   (A) dangerous
   (B) safe
   (C) rickety
   (D) scary

B.   **Shiny shoes**

   (F) glowing
   (G) clean
   (H) neat
   (J) dull

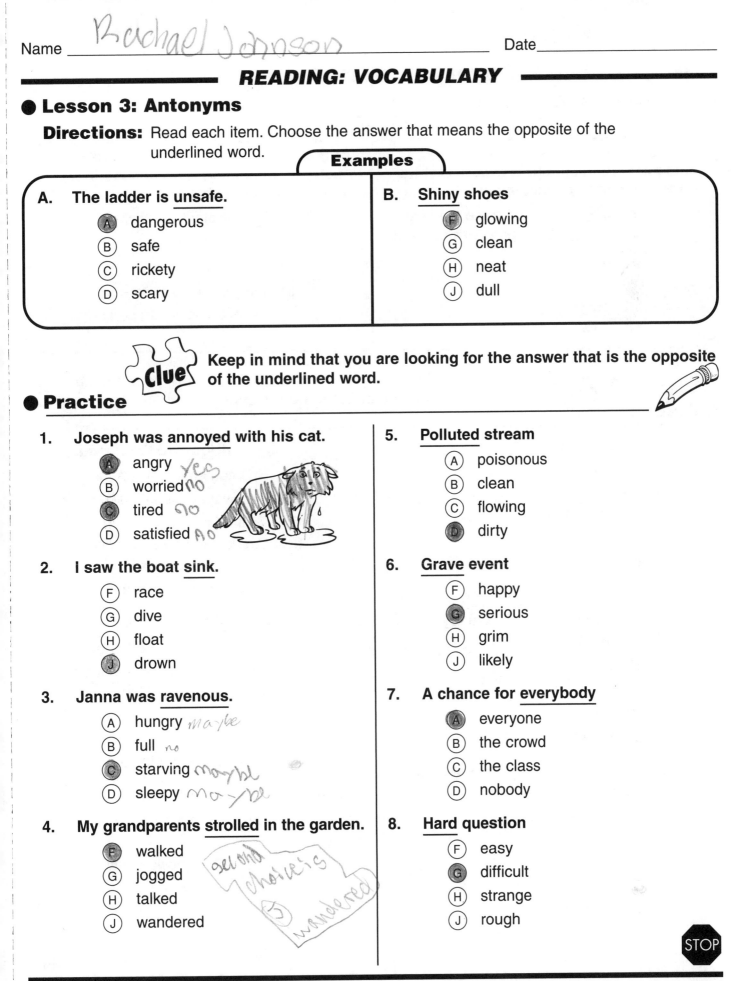

Clue Keep in mind that you are looking for the answer that is the opposite of the underlined word.

● **Practice**

1.   **Joseph was annoyed with his cat.**

   (A) angry *yes*
   (B) worried *no*
   (C) tired *no*
   (D) satisfied *no*

2.   **I saw the boat sink.**

   (F) race
   (G) dive
   (H) float
   (J) drown

3.   **Janna was ravenous.**

   (A) hungry *maybe*
   (B) full *no*
   (C) starving *maybe*
   (D) sleepy *maybe*

4.   **My grandparents strolled in the garden.**

   (F) walked
   (G) jogged
   (H) talked
   (J) wandered

   second choice is (J) wandered

5.   **Polluted stream**

   (A) poisonous
   (B) clean
   (C) flowing
   (D) dirty

6.   **Grave event**

   (F) happy
   (G) serious
   (H) grim
   (J) likely

7.   **A chance for everybody**

   (A) everyone
   (B) the crowd
   (C) the class
   (D) nobody

8.   **Hard question**

   (F) easy
   (G) difficult
   (H) strange
   (J) rough

STOP

Name _____ Date _____

READING: VOCABULARY

● **Lesson 4: Multi-Meaning Words**

For A and numbers 1–3, read the two sentences. Then choose the word that fits in the blank in both sentences.

A.   Use the _____ to make the hole.
      The _____ at the party was delicious.

   Ⓐ shovel (crossed out)
   Ⓑ dig
   ● punch
   Ⓓ rake

For B and numbers 4–6, find the answer in which the underlined word is used in the same way as in the box.

B.   This ⬚kind⬚ of plant is rare.

   Ⓕ Mrs. Rodriguez is kind.
   Ⓖ The kind man smiled.
   Ⓗ I like this kind of cereal.
   Ⓙ No one thinks that person is kind.

Clue Be careful! Only one answer is correct. Make sure your choice matches the example or fits in both blanks.

● **Practice**

1. The tree had rough _____.
    The dog wanted to _____ all the time.

    Ⓐ branches
    Ⓑ yap
    ● bark
    Ⓓ jump

2. Did the baby _____ the toy?
    Mr. Lee wanted to take a _____.

    Ⓕ sleep
    Ⓖ lose
    Ⓗ ruin
    ● break

3. Dad gets a _____ every week.
    I want to _____ my math homework.

    Ⓐ note
    Ⓑ redo
    ● check
    Ⓓ payment

4. The knight will ⬚bow⬚ to the queen.

    Ⓕ She tied a big bow on the gift.
    ● I know that I should bow to my dance partner.
    Ⓗ Did you see how the bow matched her dress?
    Ⓙ A bow is made of ribbon.

5. Put your ⬚hand⬚ on the table.

    Ⓐ Give Mr. Johnson a hand.
    Ⓑ The band deserves a hand for their music.
    Ⓒ Please give your little sister your hand.
    ● I have to hand it to you.

6. You need to do it this ⬚way⬚.

    Ⓕ The king sat way up on the throne.
    ● The recipe shows the way to make a cake.
    Ⓗ He found his way home.
    Ⓙ I don't know the way to the school.

STOP

═══ READING: READING COMPREHENSION ═══

● **Lesson 13: Recalling Details**

Directions: Read each passage. Choose the answer you believe is correct for each question.

took pos. out.

Example

Emily Ann wears a long, blue dress, a blue bonnet, and a shawl. Her head is made of china and her shoes are real leather. Emily Ann has lived with the same family for almost two hundred years. But her new owner, Betty, is forgetful. Yesterday, she left Emily Ann in the park.

A. **Which detail tells you that Emily Ann is a doll?**

- (A) Her shoes are made of leather.
- (B) She wears a shawl.
- (C) Her head is made of china.
- (D) She wears a long blue dress.

 **Clue** Skim the passage, then read the questions. Look for the specific details in phrases of the story.

● **Practice**

The Perfect Party

Ian turned on his computer and started searching the Internet for ideas. This year, he wanted to give the best Fourth of July party ever. It was Ian's favorite holiday because it was also his birthday. Ian wanted to find ideas for games and prizes. He wanted recipes for red, white, and blue food. He wanted ideas for signs and decorations. When Ian saw a Web site called "Perfect Parties for Patriots," he knew he had found exactly the right place to start his party planning.

1. **Why is the Fourth of July Ian's favorite holiday?**

- (A) Red, white, and blue are his favorite colors.
- (B) The Fourth of July is a great day for games and prizes.
- (C) The Fourth of July is Ian's birthday.
- (D) Ian is a patriot who loves his country.

2. **Which of the following things did Ian *not* look for on the Internet?**

- (F) ideas for games and prizes
- (G) recipes for red, white, and blue food
- (H) ideas for decorations
- (J) places to see firework displays

3. **What was the name of the Web site that Ian found?**

- (A) "Parties for Perfect Patriots"
- (B) "Patriot Parties"
- (C) "Perfect Parties for Patriots"
- (D) "Perfect Patriotic Parties"

STOP

READING: READING COMPREHENSION

● Lesson 14: Inferencing

Directions: Read each passage. Choose the answer you believe is correct for each question.

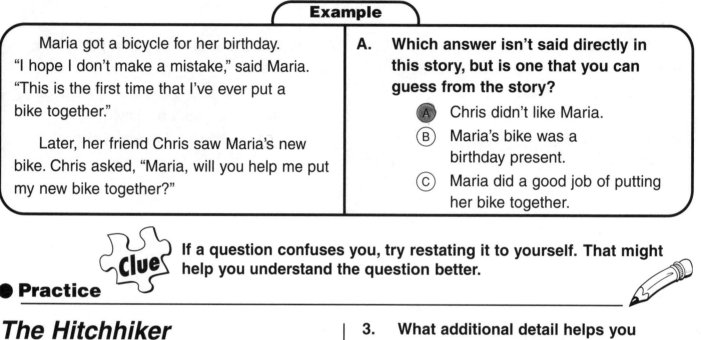

Example

Maria got a bicycle for her birthday. "I hope I don't make a mistake," said Maria. "This is the first time that I've ever put a bike together."

Later, her friend Chris saw Maria's new bike. Chris asked, "Maria, will you help me put my new bike together?"

A. **Which answer isn't said directly in this story, but is one that you can guess from the story?**

(A) Chris didn't like Maria.

(B) Maria's bike was a birthday present.

(C) Maria did a good job of putting her bike together.

Clue If a question confuses you, try restating it to yourself. That might help you understand the question better.

● Practice

The Hitchhiker

I need to go across the street,
But I'm too tired. I have eight sore feet!
I'll climb up on this person's shoe.
I'll spin a safety belt or two.
Hey! Just a minute! It's time to stop.
Please let me off at this nice shop.
Just my luck! I picked someone
Who doesn't walk—just runs and runs!

1. **Who is the speaker in this poem?**

(A) an older woman

(B) a dog

(C) a fly

(D) a spider

2. **What clue tells you about the speaker's identity?**

(F) tired

(G) needs to go across the street

(H) going shopping

(J) eight feet

3. **What additional detail helps you identify the speaker?**

(A) The speaker is small enough to ride on a shoe.

(B) The speaker is bossy.

(C) The speaker is determined to go across the street.

(D) The speaker likes to hitchhike.

4. **What can you guess from the last two lines of the poem?**

(F) The speaker spends a lot of money.

(G) The speaker goes into the store.

(H) The shoe belongs to another shopper.

(J) The shoe belongs to a jogger.

STOP

READING: READING COMPREHENSION

● **Lesson 15: Fact and Opinion**

Directions: Read each passage. Choose the answer you believe is correct for each question.

Example

It had snowed all night. "Hurray!" said Jeffrey. "No school today! Snowstorms are the greatest!"

"Not only do I have to get to work," said Mom glumly, "but I also have to shovel snow."

Candy barked. She loved to play in the snow. She was as happy as Jeffrey.

A. **Which one of these statements is an opinion?**

- Ⓐ Mom had to shovel snow.
- Ⓑ It had snowed all night.
- Ⓒ Snowstorms are the greatest.
- Ⓓ The dog was happy.

Clue To help you identify some opinions, look for words like *believe*, *feel*, and *think*.

● **Practice**

History Lesson

The students looked at the Web site about Thanksgiving. "I think that the Pilgrims were very brave," said Chad.

"When they came to Massachusetts, there were no other settlers from Europe," Keisha said. "I bet they probably felt lonely here."

"Their first year was a difficult one," Mr. Perez added. "Many of the Pilgrims became ill."

"I think I would have wanted to go home!" said Ang. "I would have felt that even boarding the *Mayflower* was a big mistake."

1. **What opinion did Keisha express?**
   - Ⓐ The Pilgrims were the only European settlers in Massachusetts.
   - Ⓑ The Pilgrims had a difficult first year.
   - Ⓒ The Pilgrims wanted to go home.
   - Ⓓ The Pilgrims probably felt lonely.

2. **What fact did Keisha state?**
   - Ⓕ The Pilgrims were the only European settlers in Massachusetts.
   - Ⓖ The Pilgrims were brave.
   - Ⓗ The Pilgrims made a mistake by boarding the *Mayflower*.
   - Ⓙ The Pilgrims had a difficult first year.

3. **Which two characters in the story expressed only opinions?**
   - Ⓐ Chad and Keisha
   - Ⓑ Mr. Perez and Keisha
   - Ⓒ Chad and Ang
   - Ⓓ Ang and Mr. Perez

4. **Which character expressed only facts?**
   - Ⓕ Chad
   - Ⓖ Keisha
   - Ⓗ Mr. Perez
   - Ⓙ Ang

READING: READING COMPREHENSION

● Lesson 16: Story Elements

Directions: Read each passage. Choose the answer you believe is correct for each question.

Example

Sara's heart pounded as she slipped the small, white envelope into the box on Joel's desk. She had not signed the pink heart inside. She looked around carefully, hoping no one had seen her.

A.   What is the setting of this story?

- Ⓐ In a classroom on Valentine's Day
- Ⓑ In a classroom on May Day
- Ⓒ In a classroom on Mother's Day
- Ⓓ On a porch on Valentine's Day

 **Clue** Keep in mind that questions about story elements can include characters, settings, plot, and problem.

● Practice

The Runner

Alanna loved to run. She ran to school and she ran home. She ran to the library and to her friends' houses. One day she ran downstairs and said, "I think I'll train for the marathon this summer to raise money for the homeless shelter." She knew that the winner would get a trophy and $1,000 for the shelter.

Alanna started to train for the marathon. She bought a new pair of running shoes. She ran on the track and on the sidewalks. After a month, her knees started to hurt. The pain got worse, and her mother took Alanna to the doctor. "You have runner's knees," said the doctor. "You have done too much running without warming up. You'll have to do some exercises to strengthen your knees."

Alanna had to slow down for a couple of weeks. As she exercised, her pain decreased. Soon she was able to run again. At the end of August, her friends stood cheering as Alanna broke the tape at the marathon.

1.   What word best describes Alanna?

- Ⓐ smart
- Ⓑ athletic
- Ⓒ musical
- Ⓓ stubborn

2.   What is the setting at the end of the story?

- Ⓕ Alanna's home
- Ⓖ the doctor's office
- Ⓗ the marathon
- Ⓙ Alanna's school

3.   What is the problem in the story?

- Ⓐ Alanna loses the marathon.
- Ⓑ Alanna runs on the sidewalk and ruins her shoes.
- Ⓒ Alanna runs in too many places and hurts her knees.
- Ⓓ Alanna runs without warming up and gets runner's knees.

STOP

READING: READING COMPREHENSION

● Lesson 17: Fiction

Directions: Read each passage. Choose the answer you believe is correct for each question.

Example

By the time the mayor came to judge the snow sculptures, Carlos had finished his. He had made a robot and had used tennis balls for eyes. "This is the most original sculpture I've seen," said the mayor. "Those are great eyes." He handed Carlos a blue ribbon.

A. How do you think Carlos feels at the end of the story?

- Ⓐ scared
- Ⓑ proud
- Ⓒ sad
- Ⓓ angry

Clue Look for key words in the story. Then look for the same key words in the questions. They will help you choose the correct answers.

● Practice

The Castle at Yule

Wyn was excited. The Great Hall was almost ready for the Yule feast. Fresh straw had been spread on the stone floor, and the tables were set with bowls, spoons, and cups. Kitchen maids hurried to bring out the food for the first course. Pipers were practicing their best music. Wyn watched as the huge Yule log was rolled into the fireplace. It would burn there for the next twelve days and nights. "Soon the feasting will start," thought Wyn, "and even I, a simple page, will be able to eat my fill. Truly this winter holiday is the best time of the whole year!"

1. This story is mostly about—

- Ⓐ a piper.
- Ⓑ a kitchen maid.
- Ⓒ a page.
- Ⓓ the lord of the castle.

2. What is set on the tables?

- Ⓕ bowls, knives, and forks
- Ⓖ plates, spoons, and cups
- Ⓗ bowls, spoons, and cups
- Ⓙ knives, forks, and spoons

3. How long do you think that Yule lasts?

- Ⓐ one day
- Ⓑ one night
- Ⓒ ten days and nights
- Ⓓ twelve days and nights

4. What opinion does Wyn express?

- Ⓕ The feasting will soon begin.
- Ⓖ Yule is the best time of the year.
- Ⓗ A page will be able to eat his fill.
- Ⓙ The Great Hall was almost ready.

Name _____   Date_____

━━━━━━━━━━ **READING: READING COMPREHENSION** ━━━━━━━━━━

● **Lesson 18: Fiction**

Directions: Read each passage. Choose the answer you believe is correct for each question.

╭─────────────── **Example** ───────────────╮

Lynn was invited to a costume party. There was going to be a prize for the funniest costume. Lynn went as a clown. When she got to the party, she looked at what the others were wearing. Lynn said, "I guess a lot of people think a clown's costume is funny!"

A. **From this story, what can you guess about the costumes at the party?**

  Ⓐ A lot of people had red and white costumes.

  Ⓑ Lynn was the only person dressed as a clown.

  Ⓒ Lynn was not the only person dressed as a clown.

  Ⓓ Most people had worn costumes.

╰──╯

Clue First, answer any easy questions whose answers you are sure that you know.

● **Practice**

Danny's Day on the Trail

Today was the day I had been dreading—our class nature hike. My mother could barely drag me out of bed. I hate being outdoors. I'd rather be in my room, zapping alien spaceships. When I'm outside, I always feel clumsy. Plus, I always get poison ivy, even if I'm miles away from the plants!

On the bus, Mr. Evans handed out lists we were supposed to fill in during our nature hike. We were supposed to write down how many animals we spotted and which rocks and leaves we could find. As if the hike itself wasn't bad enough! I lost my canteen right away. It rolled down a cliff and bounced into the river. Then I ripped my T-shirt on a bush that had huge thorns. I did manage to find a couple of the rocks on our list, but only because I tripped

on them. I am sure there wasn't a single animal anywhere on the trail. Of course, I did fall down a lot, so maybe I scared them all away.

By the time we got back to the bus, I was hot, dirty, and tired. I was so glad to get back home that I nearly hugged my computer. But by bedtime, it was clear that somehow, I had gotten poison ivy again. I was covered with it!

READING: READING COMPREHENSION

● **Lesson 18: Fiction (cont.)**

Answer the questions about the passage on page 26.

1. **What word best describes Danny's day?**
   - Ⓐ enjoyable
   - Ⓑ scary
   - Ⓒ unhappy
   - Ⓓ interesting

2. **What happened to Danny's canteen on the hike?**
   - Ⓕ It broke on a rock on the trail.
   - Ⓖ It rolled down a cliff and got lost in the woods.
   - Ⓗ It rolled down a cliff and got lost in the river.
   - Ⓙ It got left behind because Danny forgot it.

3. **What do you think is Danny's hobby?**
   - Ⓐ playing computer games
   - Ⓑ bird watching
   - Ⓒ sleeping
   - Ⓓ hiking

4. **Which of these is an opinion?**
   - Ⓕ Mr. Evans handed out lists we were supposed to fill in.
   - Ⓖ I fell down a lot.
   - Ⓗ It's so much more interesting playing computer games.
   - Ⓙ I had gotten poison ivy again.

5. **Choose the correct order of the settings for this story.**
   - Ⓐ the bus, the nature trail, the bus, Danny's home
   - Ⓑ Danny's home, the nature trail, the bus
   - Ⓒ the bus, the nature trail, the bus, Danny's classroom, Danny's home
   - Ⓓ Danny's home, the bus, the nature trail, the bus, Danny's home

6. **The boxes show some things that happened in the story. Which of these belongs in Box 2?**

Danny gets a list on the bus.	Box 2	Danny gets back on the bus.

   - Ⓕ Danny doesn't want to get out of bed.
   - Ⓖ Danny rips his T-shirt on a thorn.
   - Ⓗ Danny finds out he has poison ivy.
   - Ⓙ Danny nearly hugs his computer.

7. **Why do you think the author has Danny talk about all his problems on the trail?**
   - Ⓐ to make him seem brave
   - Ⓑ to add humor to the story
   - Ⓒ to show how much he loves hiking
   - Ⓓ to show that he talked too much

READING: READING COMPREHENSION

● Lesson 19: Fiction

Directions: Read each passage. Choose the answer you believe is correct for each question.

Example

One night in the woods, I saw a bright, white spaceship under some trees. I was scared, but I tried to be brave. I was afraid the aliens might take me away to their planet. Suddenly, the spaceship opened and my friend Paula got out. The spaceship was not a ship at all. It was just her family's camper.

A. **What surprise does the author reveal at the end?**

Ⓐ The aliens fly away again.

Ⓑ The spaceship is really a camper.

Ⓒ The speaker is just having a dream.

Ⓓ Paula is an alien.

Clue Stay with your first choice for an answer. Change it only if you are sure that another answer is better.

● Practice

The Contest

Tat and Lin loved to enter contests. It did not matter what the prize was. Once they wrote a poem for a magazine contest. They won a free copy of the magazine. Another time they guessed how many marbles were in a glass jar. They got to take all the marbles home with them.

One morning Tat was reading the Crunchy Munchies cereal box as he ate his breakfast. "Lin," he said, "here's another contest! The first-place winner gets a bike. Second prize is a tent."

"Those are great prizes," said Lin. "How do we enter?" The box said that the boys had to fill out a box top with their names and address. The more box tops they filled out, the better their chances for winning the drawing. Tat and Lin started eating Crunchy Munchies every morning. They also asked everyone they knew for cereal box tops.

By the end of four weeks, Tat and Lin had sixteen box tops to send in for the drawing. "I'm glad that's over," said Tat. "If I had to look at another box of that stuff, I don't know what I'd do."

A few weeks passed. One day, the boys got a letter in the mail. "Hooray! We've won third prize in the Crunchy Munchies contest!" Lin exclaimed. "I didn't even know there was a third prize."

Tat took the letter and started to read. His smile disappeared. "Oh, no!" he cried. "Third prize is a year's supply of Crunchy Munchies!"

GO ON

READING: READING COMPREHENSION

● Lesson 19: Fiction (cont.)

Answer the questions about the story on page 28.

1. **What is this story about?**
    - (A) two teachers who love cereal
    - (B) two cereal makers who love contests
    - (C) a pair of sisters who play marbles
    - (D) a pair of brothers who love contests

2. **How do the boys find out about the Crunchy Munchies contest?**
    - (F) from a letter in the mail
    - (G) from the back of a cereal box
    - (H) from their mother
    - (J) from their teacher

3. **Why do you think that the boys did not try to find out about the third prize before they entered the contest?**
    - (A) because the third prize was added later
    - (B) because they thought they would win first prize
    - (C) because they forgot to write and find out
    - (D) because the prizes in contests didn't really matter to them

4. **Which of these statements is a fact from the story?**
    - (F) Tat and Lin seem to dislike each other.
    - (G) Entering contests is a hobby for Tat and Lin.
    - (H) Tat and Lin will probably do anything to win first prize.
    - (J) Tat and Lin want the tent so they can go camping.

5. **What is the problem in this story?**
    - (A) Tat and Lin can't figure out how to enter the contest.
    - (B) Tat and Lin eat so much cereal they can't stand it anymore.
    - (C) Tat and Lin don't collect enough box tops to win.
    - (D) Tat and Lin argue about who will get the prize.

6. **How many cereal box tops did Tat and Lin send in?**
    - (F) sixteen
    - (G) six
    - (H) ten
    - (J) seventeen

7. **What do you think Crunchy Munchies is like?**
    - (A) smooth like pudding
    - (B) crisp and sweet
    - (C) cooked cereal like oatmeal
    - (D) salty like crackers

8. **The next thing that Tat and Lin might do is—**
    - (F) find someone to whom they can give the cereal.
    - (G) enter another Crunchy Munchies contest.
    - (H) give up contests altogether.
    - (J) have a fight over who gets the cereal.

STOP

READING: READING COMPREHENSION

● **Lesson 20: Reading Literature**

Directions: Read the story. Choose the best answers to the questions that follow.

Why the Sun and the Moon Live in the Sky

Many, many years ago in Ghana, Sun and Moon lived together on Earth. Water was their best friend, and they often went to see him. But Water never went to the house of Sun and Moon. Sun asked Water why he didn't visit. Water explained that many friends from the deep followed him everywhere. He was afraid there would be no room for them all.

So, Sun and Moon built a bigger house and invited Water to come with his friends. Water was delighted to accept, and brought along fish of all sizes, eels, crabs, whales, and every swimming creature. Soon, Water was up to Sun's head. Still, the waves rose higher and higher. At last, Water was so high in the house that Sun and Moon went to the rooftop and sat there. Water soon reached the roof.

What could Sun and Moon do? Where could they sit? They waved good-bye to Water and went up to the sky. They liked the sky so much that they decided to stay.

● **Practice**

1. **Why do Sun and Moon go to live in the sky?**

    (A) There is not enough room for them with Water and his friends in the house.

    (B) Water and his friends ask them to move.

    (C) Sun and Moon grow tired of Water and his friends.

    (D) Sun and Moon want to invite Water and his friends over to their house.

2. **The story tells**

    (F) why Water never visits Sun and Moon.

    (G) why Sun and Moon build a bigger house.

    (H) why Sun and Moon are in the sky and Water is on Earth.

    (J) why Water's many friends follow him everywhere.

GO ON

READING: READING COMPREHENSION

● Lesson 20: Reading Literature (cont.)

3. **In the phrase *friends from the deep, deep* means**
   - (A) underground.
   - (B) ocean.
   - (C) bottom of a mountain.
   - (D) dark.

4. **What is the purpose of the story?**
   - (F) to explain why Water has so many friends
   - (G) to explain why Sun and Moon build a bigger house
   - (H) to explain why Sun and Moon are in the sky
   - (J) to explain why Sun and Moon want to invite Water to their house

5. **In the title *Why the Sun and the Moon Live in the Sky*, the word *live* means**
   - (A) to be seen in the sky.
   - (B) to eat and sleep in the sky.
   - (C) to move into the sky.
   - (D) to make a home in the sky.

6. **Why does Water have so many friends?**
   - (F) He is friendly.
   - (G) He lives on Earth.
   - (H) Many creatures live in water.
   - (J) He invites them over to his house.

7. **How do Sun and Moon feel about going into the sky?**
   - (A) They are angry that Water forced them out of their home.
   - (B) They are happy because they like the sky.
   - (C) They are sad to leave their home.
   - (D) They are lonely for their best friend Water.

8. **Having Water so high in the house that Sun and Moon have to sit on the rooftop is like a**
   - (F) thunderstorm.
   - (G) drought.
   - (H) heat wave.
   - (J) flood.

9. **How do you learn about the story?**
   - (A) Sun tells the story.
   - (B) Moon tells the story.
   - (C) Water tells the story.
   - (D) A narrator tells the story.

10. **How do Sun and Moon show how they feel about Water?**
   - (F) They build a bigger home so Water could come over.
   - (G) They are angry about having to move to the sky.
   - (H) They visit Water but do not want Water to visit them.
   - (J) They sit on the roof to get away from Water.

READING: READING COMPREHENSION

● **Lesson 21: Nonfiction**

Directions: Read each passage. Choose the answer you believe is correct for each question.

Example

The light from a star has to pass through air in order for people to see the star. Air is all around the earth. As starlight travels through the air, the air moves and changes. So the starlight bends, and the star is said to twinkle.

A.   What makes a star seem to twinkle?

(A) air passing through a star

(B) starlight bending as the air moves

(C) starlight circling the star

(D) people looking at the star

 Clue Read the passage carefully and make sure you understand the facts. Then skim the article again as you answer each question.

● **Practice**

A Busy Morning

The finches are the first to arrive at the feeder. They chirp and take turns eating the seeds. Later, the doves join them. The doves almost never eat at feeders. Instead, they like to peck the seeds that have fallen to the ground. After they have eaten, they sometimes settle down near a plant in the garden to rest. Another bird that eats on the ground is the junco. Juncoes usually arrive in flocks of about ten. They are shy birds and fly away at the first sound or movement of a person in the yard. The sparrows fly to and from the feeder all morning long. They are lively birds that chirp, hop, chase each other, and go from the feeder to their home in the hedge and back again.

1.   **Another title that shows the main idea of this passage is—**

(A) "My Favorite Bird."

(B) "Juncoes and Doves."

(C) "Backyard Birds."

(D) "Sparrows in the Hedge."

2.   **Which birds like to eat on the ground?**

(F) finches and doves

(G) doves and sparrows

(H) juncoes and doves

(J) finches and sparrows

3.   **Which type of bird probably stays on the ground the longest?**

(A) finch

(B) dove

(C) junco

(D) sparrow

4.   **Which statement is a fact from the passage?**

(F) Juncoes are the most beautiful birds in the backyard.

(G) Juncoes eat seeds on the ground, not in the feeder.

(H) Juncoes usually arrive in flocks of about twenty.

(J) Juncoes seem greedy about food compared to other birds.

READING: READING COMPREHENSION

● Lesson 22: Nonfiction

Directions: Read each passage. Choose the answer you believe is correct for each question.

Example

Jellyfish come in all sizes and colors. Some are only one inch across. Other jellyfish are five feet wide. Some are orange. Others are red. Some jellyfish have no color at all. Gently poke one type of jellyfish with a stick and it will glow. But don't let any jellyfish touch you, because they can sting!

A. The main idea of this passage is—
- (A) jellyfish can sting.
- (B) some jellyfish are orange.
- (C) there are many kinds of jellyfish.
- (D) jellyfish can hide.

 **Clue** Look for key words in the story and the questions to help you choose the right answers.

● Practice

Therapy Dogs

Therapy dogs can help patients get better after illnesses. The dogs' owners bring them into hospital rooms and let patients meet the animals. Dogs sometimes go right up to patients' beds. People in the hospital rooms can pet the dogs, brush them, and talk to them. Studies have shown that being with dogs and other animals is *therapeutic*. It can lower stress, lower blood pressure, and help people heal faster.

Not every dog is a good choice for this important job. To be a therapy dog, a dog must have a calm, friendly *disposition*. Some therapy dog owners feel that their pets were born to help sick people get well again.

1. What is the main idea of this passage?
- (A) Therapy dogs like to be brushed.
- (B) Therapy dogs are calm and friendly.
- (C) Therapy dogs help patients get better after illnesses.
- (D) Therapy dogs were born to visit hospitals.

2. The word *disposition* means—
- (F) work history.
- (G) personality.
- (H) intelligence.
- (J) breed.

3. Which words help you figure out the meaning of *therapeutic*?
- (A) "sometimes go right up to patients' beds"
- (B) "lower stress, lower blood pressure, and help people heal faster"
- (C) "a calm, friendly disposition"

Name _____ Date _____

READING: READING COMPREHENSION

● Lesson 23: Nonfiction

Directions: Read each passage. Choose the answer you believe is correct for each question.

Example

Japan is very mountainous. Level areas for farming are few. Japan can farm only about 15 percent of its land. But Japan raises almost three-fourths of the food it needs to feed its people. Farmers combine up-to-date farming methods with improved seeds to make the best use of the land.

A. How much of its land can Japan farm?
- (A) 10 percent
- (B) 15 percent
- (C) two-thirds
- (D) three-fourths

Clue If you aren't sure of an answer, first decide which choices you know are wrong. Then skim the passage again to help you decide which remaining choice is the correct answer.

● Practice

Making Clay Move

Beginning in about 1990, *claymation* became very popular. *Animators* have used this clay animation to make several famous movies and TV commercials. However, claymation is not a new idea. In 1897, a claylike material called *plasticine* was invented. Moviemakers used plasticine to create clay animation films as early as 1908. Animators could use the plasticine models for scenes that could not be filmed in real life.

Here's how claymation works. First, an artist makes one or more clay models. Moviemakers pose each model, take a picture, and then stop. Next, they move the model a tiny bit to a slightly different pose. Then they take another picture. They continue the pattern of taking pictures, moving the model, and taking pictures again. It can take hundreds of pictures to make a few seconds of film. The idea of moving models and using stop-action photography came from a French animator named George Melier. He had once had a job as a magician and called his work "trick film."

Today's animators use different kinds of clay. They can also use computers to speed up the claymation process. But the basic idea of clay animation has not changed in over a hundred years!

GO ON

READING: READING COMPREHENSION

● **Lesson 23: Nonfiction (cont.)**

Answer the questions about the passage on page 34.

1. This story is mostly about—

(A) the history of claymation films.

(B) George Melier, a French magician.

(C) making models out of plasticine.

(D) today's animators and how they work.

2. When was the first claymation movie made?

(F) 1990

(G) 1908

(H) 1897

(J) 1920

3. What do you think "stop-action photography" is?

(A) making everyone stop while a photo is taken

(B) moving a model, taking the picture, then moving the model again

(C) using magic tricks to make the camera work

(D) a camera that stops after the picture is taken

4. Which of these choices is a fact?

(F) Claymation movies are funnier than live-action movies.

(G) Claymation movies are more interesting than other movies.

(H) Claymation movies weren't very good until the 1990s.

(J) Claymation movies were first made in 1908.

5. What is an animator?

(A) someone who works with actors

(B) someone who makes clay sculptures

(C) someone who invents clay materials

(D) someone who makes animated films

6. Who was George Melier?

(F) a filmmaker who became a magician

(G) a magician who became an animator

(H) a clay-model maker who liked to play tricks

(J) the inventor of plasticine

7. Which two words are used to make the word claymation?

(A) clay and movement

(B) clay and maker

(C) clay and animation

(D) clay and photography

8. The author wrote this passage to—

(F) entertain readers with funny stories of filmmaking.

(G) inform readers about the claymation process.

(H) make readers want to rent specific videotapes.

(J) tell the history of plasticine.

READING: READING COMPREHENSION

● Lesson 24: Reading Informational Text

Directions: Read the article. Choose the best answers for the questions that follow.

One Great Wall

A wall has many uses. It may hold things in. It may keep things out. The purpose of China's Great Wall was to keep people out. Tribes of people wanted to move across China's northern mountains and down into China. China's emperors preferred to keep those people out. So, four different walls started going up as early as 700 BC.

About 500 years later, the **emperor** got tired of fighting off the northern tribes. He wanted to connect the four main sections of the wall that had already been built. He sent thousands of peasants, poor people who did not have farms, to work on the wall. Soldiers were there to make sure the peasants stayed and worked. The peasants did work hard, and many of them died.

Then, 1,500 years after that, another emperor wanted to make the wall even stronger. He started a program that lasted more than 200 years! The wall got longer, and **watchtowers** and cannons were added at points all along the length of the wall.

A view of the Great Wall of China

In spite of the wall, China suffered a number of **invasions** over the years. The wall should have been built higher and stronger to keep invaders out. Still, the wall's size and the human effort that went into it earn it a place on the list of greatest human feats.

To learn more about China, visit https://www.cia.gov/library/publications/the-world-factbook/geos/ch.html.

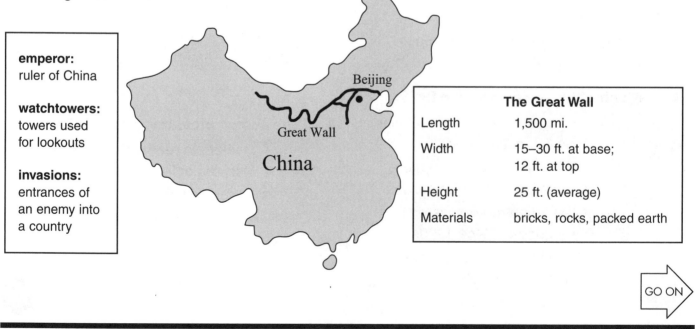

emperor: ruler of China	
watchtowers: towers used for lookouts	
invasions: entrances of an enemy into a country	

The Great Wall

Length	1,500 mi.
Width	15–30 ft. at base; 12 ft. at top
Height	25 ft. (average)
Materials	bricks, rocks, packed earth

GO ON

READING: READING COMPREHENSION

● Lesson 24: Reading Informational Text (cont.)

1. **How was the Great Wall first built?**

   (A) Watchtowers and cannons were added.

   (B) Four main sections were connected.

   (C) The wall was built stronger.

   (D) Four different walls went up.

2. **How many total years did it take to build the Great Wall of China?**

   (F) about 500 years

   (G) about 200 years

   (H) about 2,000 years

   (J) about 1,500 years

3. **What were the rulers of China called?**

   (A) emperors

   (B) tribes

   (C) soldiers

   (D) peasants

4. **What does the Web site https://www.cia.gov/library/publications/the-world-factbook/geos/ch.html give you?**

   (F) only information about the Great Wall

   (G) only information about the emperors of China

   (H) more information about maps

   (J) more information about China

5. **What is the reason for writing this selection?**

   (A) to explain

   (B) to persuade

   (C) to entertain

   (D) to learn

6. **What does the writer think should have been done to keep invaders out?**

   (F) Peace should have been made with the invaders.

   (G) The wall should have been built higher and stronger.

   (H) More soldiers should have been hired to make the peasants work.

   (J) The four sections of the wall should have been connected.

7. **From the map, you can see that the Great Wall was built to keep out invaders from**

   (A) the ocean on the east coast of China.

   (B) the north.

   (C) the west.

   (D) the south.

8. **What can you learn about the Great Wall from looking at the photo?**

   (F) It is in a desert.

   (G) It is by the ocean.

   (H) It is in a swamp.

   (J) It is in the mountains.

Name _____   Date_____

Directions: Read each item. Choose the answer you believe is correct for each question.

Example

When it stopped raining, Keisha began walking home. Soon she came to a big puddle in the middle of the sidewalk. Keisha ran toward the puddle and jumped high in the air. After she landed, Keisha said, "Oh! I guess I should have walked around that puddle!"

A. Why did Keisha think she should have walked around the puddle?

(A) because she didn't have boots
(B) because the puddle water splashed on her
(C) because it was still raining
(D) because she loved puddles

For numbers 1–8, read the passage. Choose the answer you believe is correct for each question.

Wendy Lost and Found

Wendy was scared. For the second time in her young life, she was lost. When the branch fell on her small house and the fence, she had barely escaped. She leaped across the fallen fence into the woods. Now the rain poured down and the wind howled. The little woodchuck shivered under a big oak tree. She did not know what to do.

When Wendy was a baby, her mother had died. She had been alone in the woods then, too. She could not find enough food. Then she hurt her paw. All day she scratched at a small hole in the ground, trying to make a burrow. Every night, she was hungry.

One day, Rita had found her. Rita had knelt down by Wendy's shallow burrow and set down an apple. Wendy limped slowly out and took the apple. It was the best thing she had ever tasted. Rita took the baby woodchuck to the wildlife center, and Wendy had lived there ever since. Most of the animals at the center were orphans. Rita taught them how to live in the wild, and then let them go when they were ready. But Wendy's

paw did not heal well, and Rita knew that Wendy would never be able to go back to the wild. So Rita had made Wendy a house and a pen. Wendy even had a job—she visited schools with Rita so that students could learn all about woodchucks.

Now the storm had ruined Wendy's house. She did not know how to find Rita. At dawn, the rain ended. Wendy limped down to a big stream and sniffed the air. Maybe the center was across the stream. Wendy jumped onto a rock and then hopped to another one. She landed on her bad paw and fell into the fast-moving water. The little woodchuck struggled to keep her nose above water. The current tossed her against a tangle of branches. Wendy held on with all her might.

"There she is!" Wendy heard Rita's voice. Rita and Ben, another worker from the wildlife center, were across the stream. Rita waded out to the branches, lifted Wendy up, and wrapped her in a blanket. Wendy purred her thanks. By the time Ben and Rita got into the van to go back to the center, Wendy was fast asleep.

GO ON

READING: READING COMPREHENSION
SAMPLE TEST (cont.)

Answer the questions about the story on page 38.

1. This story is mostly about—

- (A) a wildlife center worker.
- (B) a woodchuck who lives at a wildlife center.
- (C) a woodchuck who can do tricks.
- (D) a woodchuck who learns how to swim.

2. How does the story start?

- (F) with Wendy's life as a baby
- (G) in the middle of the storm
- (H) with Wendy's visit to school
- (J) when Wendy is in the stream

3. Why do you think the author wrote about Wendy's life as a baby?

- (A) so the reader knows that Wendy has been lost before and knows what to do
- (B) so the reader knows that Wendy can't live in the wild and is in danger
- (C) so the reader knows that Wendy trusts people and will be all right
- (D) so the reader knows that Wendy can find apples to eat

4. Which answer is a fact about woodchucks from the story?

- (F) Wendy loves apples.
- (G) Woodchucks dig burrows.
- (H) Woodchucks can climb tall fences.
- (J) Wendy limps because of her hurt paw.

5. What is the problem in the story "Wendy Lost and Found"?

- (A) Wendy hurt her paw.
- (B) Wendy got lost as a baby.
- (C) Wendy gets lost during a big storm.
- (D) Wendy does not trust Ben.

6. What are the settings for this story?

- (F) the woods and the wildlife center
- (G) the school and the stream
- (H) the school and the woods
- (J) the wildlife center and Rita's house

7. What is Rita's job?

- (A) saving woodchucks from streams
- (B) teaching science at a school
- (C) gathering apples
- (D) working at the wildlife center with animals

8. What is the climax of the story?

- (F) when Wendy's mother dies
- (G) when Rita gives Wendy an apple
- (H) when Wendy falls into the stream
- (J) when Rita wraps Wendy in a blanket

GO ON

READING: READING COMPREHENSION
SAMPLE TEST (cont.)

Directions: Read each item. Choose the answer you believe is correct for each question.

Example

The Mayan people of Mexico and Central America played an early form of basketball. Their "hoop" was made of stone. The opening was set at a right angle to the ground, like a window in a house. This opening was much higher than today's basketball hoops.

B. What was one difference between the Mayan basketball game and ours?

- (A) The Mayan court was much longer.
- (B) The game lasted a shorter time.
- (C) The hoop was made of stone instead of metal.
- (D) The game was played inside a house.

For numbers 9–15, read the passage. Choose the answer you believe is correct for each question.

The Forgotten Flyer

In 1908, Jacqueline Cochran was born to a poor family in Pensacola, Florida. Like many girls at the time, she went to work at an early age. When she was just eight years old, Jacqueline started work in a cotton mill. As she worked on the looms, making cloth, she dreamed about becoming an aviator. She wanted to fly one of the airplanes that had been recently invented.

Jacqueline got her wish in the 1930s. She became a pilot at a time when airplanes were being avoided by most people. Only a handful of daring young men flew these new planes, and there were very few women aviators. That did not stop Jacqueline. She took flying lessons and began to enter famous races. In 1938, she won first prize in a contest to fly across the United States.

At the beginning of World War II, Jacqueline trained women in England as pilots. She later came back to the United States and trained American women, too. In 1945, she was awarded the Distinguished Service Medal, one of America's highest honors.

When jet planes were invented, Jacqueline learned to fly them, too. Soon, she was the first woman to fly faster than the speed of sound. Jacqueline also set many other records in the field of aviation, including flying higher than anyone had before her.

In many ways, Jacqueline Cochran is forgotten today. But this woman pilot should be remembered. She was a pioneer in a new technology. She helped to make air travel one of our most important means of transportation.

Answer the questions about the passage on page 40.

9. **This story is mostly about—**

   (A) a brave pioneer in the field of air travel.

   (B) a weaver who becomes a teacher.

   (C) a soldier who wins the Distinguished Service Medal.

   (D) a founder of an important mill business.

10. **What is an aviator?**

    (F) a weaver

    (G) a woman

    (H) a pilot

    (J) a teacher

11. **This story suggests that—**

    (A) jet planes were invented in about 1908.

    (B) Jacqueline Cochran founded an airline.

    (C) many people were flying by 1930.

    (D) early airplanes were dangerous to fly.

12. **Which of the following choices is an opinion?**

    (F) Jacqueline Cochran is probably the greatest of women aviators.

    (G) Jacqueline Cochran won the Distinguished Service Medal.

    (H) Jacqueline Cochran was born in 1908.

    (J) Jacqueline Cochran learned how to fly jet planes.

13. **The boxes show events in the story. Which of these belong in Box 2?**

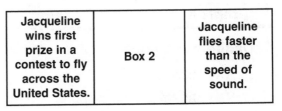

Jacqueline wins first prize in a contest to fly across the United States.	Box 2	Jacqueline flies faster than the speed of sound.

   (A) Jacqueline trains women pilots during World War II.

   (B) Jacqueline works in a cotton mill.

   (C) Jacqueline flies higher than anyone before her.

   (D) Jacqueline starts flying lessons.

14. **Why did the author title the story "The Forgotten Flyer"?**

    (F) because Jacqueline Cochran forgot about her efforts

    (G) because Jacqueline Cochran is not well known today

    (H) because Jacqueline Cochran never won a medal

    (J) because Jacqueline Cochran never set a record

15. **Cotton is a kind of a fabric. Another fabric is—**

    (A) paper.

    (B) honeycomb.

    (C) silk.

    (D) oak.

STOP

READING PRACTICE TEST

● Part 1: Vocabulary

Directions: Read each item. Choose the answer that means the same or the opposite of the underlined word.

Examples

A. **Dangerous** bridge
- (A) careful
- (B) unsafe
- (C) unpainted
- (D) deep

B. She passed an **important** test.
- (F) major
- (G) bad
- (H) general
- (J) emergency

For numbers 1–5, read each item. Choose the answer that means the same or about the same as the underlined word.

1. **Fearless** dog
- (A) careless
- (B) energetic
- (C) unafraid
- (D) sincere

2. **Solar** energy
- (F) sun-powered
- (G) sunburn
- (H) sometimes
- (J) powerful

3. **Ancient** castle
- (A) strong
- (B) bridge
- (C) stone
- (D) old

4. The train had only one **passenger**.
- (F) ticket
- (G) car
- (H) rider
- (J) conductor

5. He started on his **trip** .
- (A) holiday
- (B) class
- (C) journey
- (D) future

For numbers 6–8, read each item. Choose the answer that means the opposite of the underlined word.

6. He decided to **continue**.
- (F) stop
- (G) go on
- (H) roost
- (J) sleep

7. She was a **mighty** warrior.
- (A) great
- (B) strong
- (C) famous
- (D) weak

8. The doctor **comforted** his patient.
- (F) bothered
- (G) cheered
- (H) recognized
- (J) calmed

GO ON

For numbers 9–13, read the two sentences. Then choose the word that fits in the blank in both sentences.

9. Everyone in the class was _____.
   She picked out a nice birthday _____.

   Ⓐ quiet
   Ⓑ present
   Ⓒ comfortable
   Ⓓ gift

10. I did not shed a _____ over my lost paper.
    Mom will mend the _____ in my jacket.

    Ⓕ tear
    Ⓖ thread
    Ⓗ break
    Ⓙ banner

11. Dad broke a marathon _____ in the race.
    I want to _____ my thoughts in a diary.

    Ⓐ note
    Ⓑ record
    Ⓒ write
    Ⓓ tape

12. The _____ was worth one point.
    The _____ of the class is to learn about Native Americans.

    Ⓕ note
    Ⓖ purpose
    Ⓗ touchdown
    Ⓙ goal

13. Everyone's _____ on the field trip was great.
    She wants to _____ the orchestra.

    Ⓐ job
    Ⓑ position
    Ⓒ conduct
    Ⓓ tape

For numbers 14–16, find the answer in which the underlined word is used in the same way as in the box.

14. The ⬚field⬚ is planted with corn.

    Ⓕ The field of technology is always changing.
    Ⓖ We can see deer in the field by our house.
    Ⓗ Her field is nursing.
    Ⓙ Our field trip is next Thursday.

15. The ⬚general⬚ idea was to weave a basket.

    Ⓐ She is a general in the army.
    Ⓑ The soldiers followed their general into battle.
    Ⓒ I think that the general had the best idea.
    Ⓓ No general study of history can cover everything.

16. She wants the same ⬚type⬚ of coat.

    Ⓕ Akiko can type very fast.
    Ⓖ Let me type up this report.
    Ⓗ I like this type of cereal the best.
    Ⓙ He has to type in new data all the time.

GO ON

READING PRACTICE TEST
Part 1: Vocabulary (cont.)

For numbers 17–22, choose the answer that fits best in the blank.

17. The _____ waiter dropped the tray.

   - (A) careless
   - (B) dull
   - (C) living
   - (D) complete

18. Brave _____ circled the globe.

   - (F) dogs
   - (G) travelers
   - (H) trains
   - (J) honors

19. The wild _____ escaped from the net.

   - (A) pupil
   - (B) driver
   - (C) beast
   - (D) spider

20. Our field trip to the _____ was interesting.

   - (F) backyard
   - (G) upstairs
   - (H) traffic
   - (J) museum

21. The _____ crowed at dawn.

   - (A) lion
   - (B) giraffe
   - (C) rooster
   - (D) sparrow

22. We squeezed down a _____ hallway.

   - (F) wooden
   - (G) narrow
   - (H) foolish
   - (J) prize

For numbers 23–25, find the word that means the same thing as the underlined word.

23. The dinner was excellent. Excellent means—

   - (A) very good
   - (B) above
   - (C) higher
   - (D) unpleasant

24. No one could capture the wild tiger. Capture means—

   - (F) range
   - (G) hunt
   - (H) catch
   - (J) release

25. We need his pitching skill on our team. Skill means—

   - (A) toss
   - (B) curve
   - (C) dance
   - (D) talent

STOP

READING PRACTICE TEST

● Part 2: Reading Comprehension

Directions: Read the passage. Choose the answer you believe is correct for each question.

Example

Elsie had to walk more than a mile to school, and she was only halfway there. Her boots were wet. The shawl that her mother had wrapped over her patched coat was not keeping Elsie warm.

A. **What kind of day is described in this passage?**
- (A) sunny and warm
- (B) dry and hot
- (C) rainy and cold
- (D) cold and dry

For numbers 1–3, read the passage. Choose the answer you believe is correct for each question.

The Surprise

Tracy had a cocoon in a jar that she kept in the garage. She had found the cocoon on a bush. Tracy decided to take her cocoon to school. After all, the class had a white rat, a turtle, and three goldfish. Now they could have a butterfly, too! Tracy knew Ms. Carr would not mind an addition to the class.

"Are you sure that a butterfly will come out of this cocoon, Tracy?" asked Ms. Carr when Tracy showed her the jar.

"Oh, yes, I'm sure," Tracy answered. "And I think it will hatch any day now."

Two days later, Tracy was the first student in the classroom. She ran to the jar. Inside was a large, gray insect with a thick, furry body. "What is it?" Tracy asked, wrinkling her nose.

Ms. Carr smiled. "It's a moth," she said. "See how its wings are open while it's resting. Let's take this moth outside and watch it try its wings!"

1. **This story is mostly about—**
- (A) a girl who wants to raise turtles.
- (B) a girl who is surprised when a cocoon hatches into a moth.
- (C) a teacher who likes moths.
- (D) a teacher who is disappointed to see a moth in a jar.

2. **This story suggests that—**
- (F) both butterflies and moths hatch from cocoons.
- (G) butterflies are difficult to raise.
- (H) all children like animals and insects.
- (J) teachers should not have animals in classrooms.

3. **Which of these statements is a fact from the story?**
- (A) Ms. Carr is a substitute teacher.
- (B) Ms. Carr seems uninterested in her students.
- (C) Ms. Carr is an animal lover.
- (D) Ms. Carr must not like moths.

GO ON

Name _____ Date _____

For numbers 4–7, read the passage. Choose the answer you believe is correct for each question.

Birthday Party Blues

My birthday party was supposed to be outside, so of course it was raining. All of my guests were soaking wet. My presents were soaking wet, too. I had planned some games, but my friends were acting strangely. They kept whispering to each other all through the party games.

When it was time to open my presents, it turned out that all seven of my friends had bought me the same gift! How many copies of *Map Zap* software does one person need? It was hard to keep saying "thank you" and sound grateful each time. My friends seemed to think that the whole thing was really funny. They could not stop snickering.

Then it was time to open my present from my parents. Mom handed me a gift, and I ripped off the paper. *Map Zap* again! But Mom grinned and said, "Look inside, Darcy." Inside the box was a photograph of a puppy sitting in front of a pile of gifts. Underneath the picture, it said, "I'm waiting in the garage." I raced outside in the rain to the garage door. There was my new puppy, Snoopy, and the real gifts my friends had bought me. What a great party!

4. **What is the main idea of this story?**
   - (F) a birthday party that seems to go badly
   - (G) a little dog who goes to a birthday party
   - (H) a joke played by Darcy on her friends
   - (J) a party takes place inside because of rain

5. **What is *Map Zap*?**
   - (A) a history book
   - (B) computer software
   - (C) a book about maps
   - (D) a board game

6. **Why do you think Darcy's friends were whispering during the games?**
   - (F) because the games were strange
   - (G) because they were winning all the prizes
   - (H) because they were all going to play a joke on Darcy
   - (J) because they liked talking

7. **Which of the following is an opinion?**
   - (A) Darcy received a puppy as a gift.
   - (B) This had to be Darcy's best birthday ever.
   - (C) Darcy got eight copies of *Map Zap*.
   - (D) Darcy's party was supposed to be outside.

GO ON

READING PRACTICE TEST
Part 2: Reading Comprehension (cont.)

For numbers 8–13, read the passage. Choose the answer you believe is correct for each question.

Up, Up, and Away

Jamal climbed into the basket on that cold morning, and he shivered. The basket tipped from side to side, and he gasped. While Dad was climbing into the basket, the pilot twisted something and fire shot up into the air. Jamal jumped.

"It's all right," said the pilot. "I'm doing this to heat the air in the balloon." Jamal tipped back his head. High above him was the opening of the huge, bright balloon. He looked over the edge of the basket. The basket was tied with ropes to keep it close to the ground. But suddenly, it started to rock and rise up.

"Here we go!" said Dad, and smiled happily at Jamal.

Jamal bit his lip. "I'm not sure I am going to like this," he said.

People on the ground untied the ropes, and the balloon with its basket of passengers kept rising up into the air. It wasn't like taking off in an airplane. Instead, the balloon was floating up gently into the morning sky.

Soon Jamal, Dad, and the pilot could see far across the trees. "Look, there's the lake!" said Dad. Jamal saw a blue patch on the ground. Big Lake was suddenly tiny! The trees looked like green cotton balls. The fields looked like pieces of a quilt.

As the balloon floated on, Jamal felt less and less afraid. He started pointing at things, too. "Look, Dad, there's my school! And there's our house!" Jamal could see his treehouse in the backyard, and the shed where he kept his bicycle. The whole house and yard looked smaller than one of his thumbnails. Then Jamal looked ahead into the blue sky. The sun was starting to shine. It was the perfect day to fly in a hot-air balloon.

GO ON

READING PRACTICE TEST
Part 2: Reading Comprehension (cont.)

Answer the questions about the passage on page 47.

8. This story is mostly about—

  (F) a boy who sees his school from the air.

  (G) a boy and his father who learn about flight.

  (H) a boy and his father who fly in a hot-air balloon.

  (J) a boy and his father who learn how to fly.

9. **Jamal's house and yard look smaller than—**

  (A) the lake.

  (B) the balloon.

  (C) the trees.

  (D) his thumbnail.

10. **How can you tell Jamal is nervous at first?**

  (F) He climbs into the basket and looks at the ground.

  (G) He gasps, jumps, and bites his lip.

  (H) He smiles at his father.

  (J) He sees his school and his house.

11. **Which of these statements is an opinion?**

  (A) "I'm doing this to heat the air in the balloon."

  (B) "Here we go!"

  (C) "I'm not sure I am going to like this."

  (D) "Look, there's the lake!"

12. **Choose a word to best describe Dad's feeling about the balloon ride.**

  (F) worried

  (G) quiet

  (H) excited

  (J) interested

13. **Choose another title for this passage.**

  (A) "My House and Yard"

  (B) "Hot-Air Balloon History"

  (C) "Jamal's Balloon Ride"

  (D) "Fast Flying"

GO ON

READING PRACTICE TEST
Part 2: Reading Comprehension (cont.)

For numbers 14–19, read the passage. Choose the answer you believe is correct for each question.

Johnny Appleseed

There are many tall tales about the life of Johnny Appleseed. But the facts may surprise you!

There was a real Johnny Appleseed. His name was John Chapman. He grew up with his nine brothers and sisters in Longmeadow, Massachusetts. John always loved trees and wild animals. When he was 23 years old, John began walking west, carrying only a gun, hatchet, and knapsack. He walked over 300 miles. Sometimes he wore shoes, but sometimes he walked barefoot.

As he passed the cider mills in eastern Pennsylvania, John asked if he could have some of the mill's apple seeds. Then he found a piece of empty land and planted the seeds. He did this several times in Ohio and Indiana, too. When the seeds grew into saplings, John went back to dig up the young trees. Then he sold them to pioneers who were starting farms. These settlers wanted apples to make apple butter, cider, and vinegar. John gave away saplings for free to people who wanted the trees but were too poor to pay for them.

As John walked from place to place, he brought not only trees, but news, stories, and books. When he stayed with a family, he would read to them and then lend them books.

John lived until the age of 71. By the time he died, he left behind 15,000 apple trees and over 2,000 saplings for pioneer families to enjoy.

READING PRACTICE TEST
Part 2: Reading Comprehension (cont.)

Answer the questions about the passage on page 49.

14. Another title that shows the main idea of this passage is—

- (F) "John Chapman, Hiker."
- (G) "The Man Who Walked Across America."
- (H) "How Apple Trees Went East."
- (J) "John Chapman, The Apple-Tree Man."

15. How many apple trees did John Chapman leave behind?

- (A) 300
- (B) 2,000
- (C) 15,000
- (D) 50,000

16. Why do you think that John Chapman grew trees?

- (F) because he loved trees and could also earn a living growing them
- (G) because he wanted to eat apples all the time
- (H) because he wanted to make a lot of money
- (J) because he wanted to create more forests

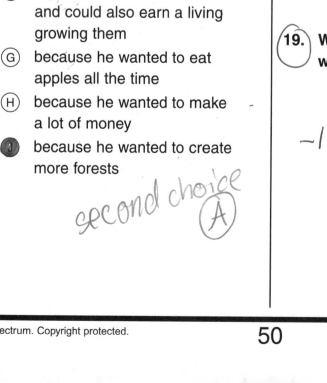

second choice (A)

17. Choose a correct fact from the passage.

- (A) John Chapman planted trees all over America.
- (B) John Chapman brought apple trees to Pennsylvania, Ohio, and Indiana.
- (C) John Chapman planted over 100,000 trees in his lifetime.
- (D) John Chapman was not able to read.

18. Which of these does this story lead you to believe?

- (F) John Chapman played a big part in helping pioneer families.
- (G) John Chapman probably did not like books very much.
- (H) John Chapman died a very rich man.
- (J) John Chapman was an unhappy person.

19. What is the meaning of the word *sapling*?

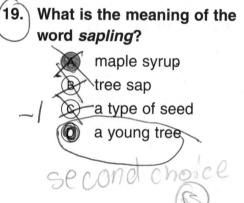

- (A) maple syrup
- (B) tree sap
- (C) a type of seed
- (D) a young tree

second choice (B)

GO ON

978-1-62057-595-6 *Spectrum Test Practice 3*

READING PRACTICE TEST
Part 2: Reading Comprehension (cont.)

For numbers 20–23, read the passage. Choose the answer you believe is correct for each question.

Sign Language

Sign language is used by people who are not able to hear or speak well. They use their hands instead of their voices to talk. Their hand signals may be different letters, words, or whole ideas.

Sign language is used by other people, too. Have you ever watched a football or basketball game? The referees use hand signals to let people know what has happened in the game. Signs can mean "foul," "time out," or can let players know when a play was good.

Guess who else uses sign language? You do! You wave your hand for *hello* and *goodbye*. You nod your head up and down to say *yes* and back and forth to say *no*. You point to show which way to go. Sign language is used by people everywhere as another way of talking.

20. What is the main idea of this passage?

(F) Sign language is used by people who cannot hear well.

(G) Sign language is important to many sports.

(H) Sign language is not used in all countries.

(J) Sign language is used by people everywhere.

21. Which are examples of sign language?

(A) calling out the name of your friend

(B) singing a song

(C) waving *hello* or *goodbye*

(D) talking on the telephone

22. Which one is another example of sign language?

(F) rocking a baby to sleep

(G) raising your hand in class

(H) running down the sidewalk to school

(J) jumping rope

23. Which one is an opinion?

(A) Sign language is used as another way of talking.

(B) Sign language is very interesting.

(C) Sign language is used in sports.

(D) Sign language is done with hand signals.

Name _____ Date _____

LANGUAGE: LANGUAGE MECHANICS

● **Lesson 1: Capitalization**

Examples

For A and numbers 1–3, choose the answer that shows a capital letter that is missing. If no capital letters are missing, choose the answer "None."

A.
- (A) The snow
- (B) started to fall
- (C) in December.
- (D) None

For B and numbers 4–5, choose the answer that shows the correct capitalization.

B. My last teacher was _____.
- (F) ms. smith
- (G) Ms. smith
- (H) Ms. Smith
- (J) ms. Smith

Clue Remember that sentences and proper nouns start with capital letters.

● **Practice**

1.
- (A) she went
- (B) to the basement
- (C) to get the laundry.
- (D) None

2.
- (F) My favorite
- (G) book is
- (H) *charlotte's Web.*
- (J) None

3.
- (A) My family
- (B) went on a trip
- (C) to ohio.
- (D) None

4. **Did you go to the game on _____?**
- (F) saturday afternoon
- (G) Saturday afternoon
- (H) Saturday Afternoon
- (J) saturday Afternoon

5. **Angela is my _____.**
- (A) favorite cousin
- (B) Favorite cousin
- (C) favorite Cousin
- (D) Favorite Cousin

STOP

Published by Spectrum. Copyright protected.   978-1-62057-595-6 *Spectrum Test Practice 3*

Name _____ Date _____

LANGUAGE: LANGUAGE MECHANICS

● Lesson 2: Punctuation

Examples

For A and numbers 1–3, choose the answer that shows the correct punctuation mark. If no punctuation marks are missing, choose the answer "None."

A. How many people were at the party?

- (A) .
- (B) ,
- (C) !
- (D) None

For B and numbers 4–5, choose the answer that shows the correct punctuation.

B. The cake _____ in the oven.

- (F) wasn't
- (G) wasn't'
- (H) wasnt
- (J) was'nt

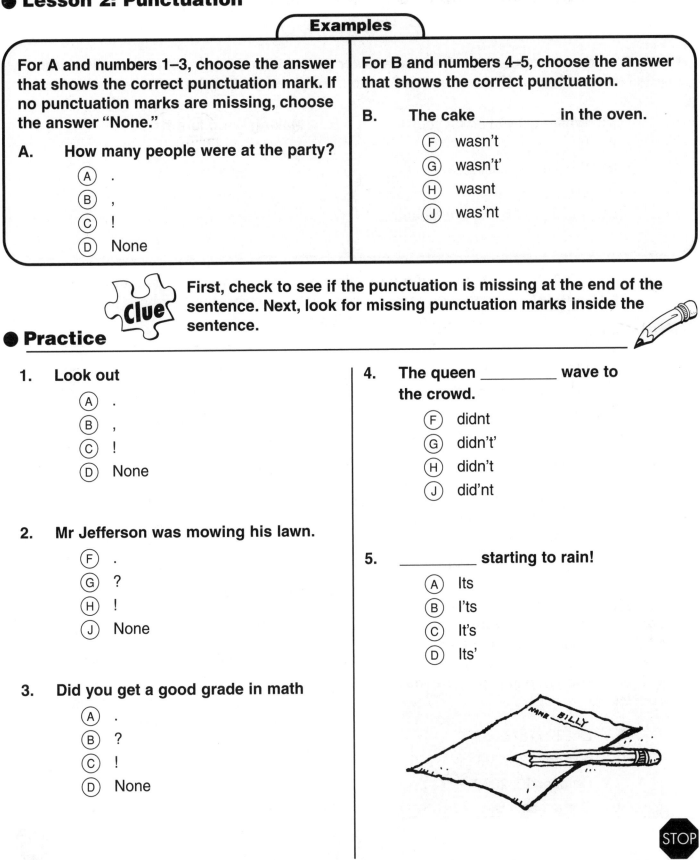

Clue First, check to see if the punctuation is missing at the end of the sentence. Next, look for missing punctuation marks inside the sentence.

● Practice

1. Look out

- (A) .
- (B) ,
- (C) !
- (D) None

2. Mr Jefferson was mowing his lawn.

- (F) .
- (G) ?
- (H) !
- (J) None

3. Did you get a good grade in math

- (A) .
- (B) ?
- (C) !
- (D) None

4. The queen _____ wave to the crowd.

- (F) didnt
- (G) didn't'
- (H) didn't
- (J) did'nt

5. _____ starting to rain!

- (A) Its
- (B) I'ts
- (C) It's
- (D) Its'

STOP

Name _____ Date_____

● **Lesson 3: Capitalization and Punctuation**

Examples

For A, B, and numbers 1–2, choose the answer that shows the correct punctuation and capitalization. Choose "Correct as it is" if the underlined part of the sentence is correct.

A.
- Ⓐ Where did you go on your vacation.
- Ⓑ We went to california.
- Ⓒ Did you like it.
- Ⓓ Yes, it was sunny and beautiful.

B. Making soup <u>isnt</u> hard.
- Ⓕ isnt'
- Ⓖ is'nt
- Ⓗ isn't
- Ⓙ Correct as it is

Clue

First, check the capitalization in the sentence. Then look for punctuation errors. Choose the answer that has both correct capitalization and punctuation.

● **Practice**

1.
- Ⓐ What is your favorite city
- Ⓑ I like San francisco.
- Ⓒ It's in California.
- Ⓓ It's where you can find the golden gate Bridge.

2.
- Ⓕ Nobody answered the door
- Ⓖ knock on the back door.
- Ⓗ Oh, no!
- Ⓙ We woke up mrs. Perez.

For numbers 3–5, read the letter. Then choose the answer that shows the correct capitalization and punctuation for the underlined phrase. Choose "Correct as it is" if the underlined part of the sentence is correct.

3.
- Ⓐ October, 12 2003
- Ⓑ october 12, 2003
- Ⓒ October 12, 2003
- Ⓓ Correct as it is

4.
- Ⓕ rowndale elementary School
- Ⓖ Rowndale Elementary school
- Ⓗ Rowndale Elementary School
- Ⓙ Correct as it is

5.
- Ⓐ Very truly yours,
- Ⓑ Very Truly Yours
- Ⓒ Very Truly yours,
- Ⓓ Correct as it is

October 12 2003

Dear Akiko,

    Please come to the Fall Festival at <u>rowndale Elementary School</u>. We will have games, prizes, and lots of snacks! It starts at noon on Saturday.

<u>Very truly Yours</u>

Ms. Michaels

STOP

LANGUAGE: LANGUAGE MECHANICS

● **Lesson 4: Using Commas**

Directions: Choose the correction for each error.

Examples

A. One person's trash is another person's treasure," I always say.

- Ⓐ treasure" I
- Ⓑ say."
- Ⓒ "One
- Ⓓ treasure, I

B. Library of Congress
101, Independence Avenue
Washington, DC 20540

- Ⓕ 101 Independence
- Ⓖ Avenue, Washington
- Ⓗ Independence, Avenue
- Ⓙ DC, 20540

● **Practice**

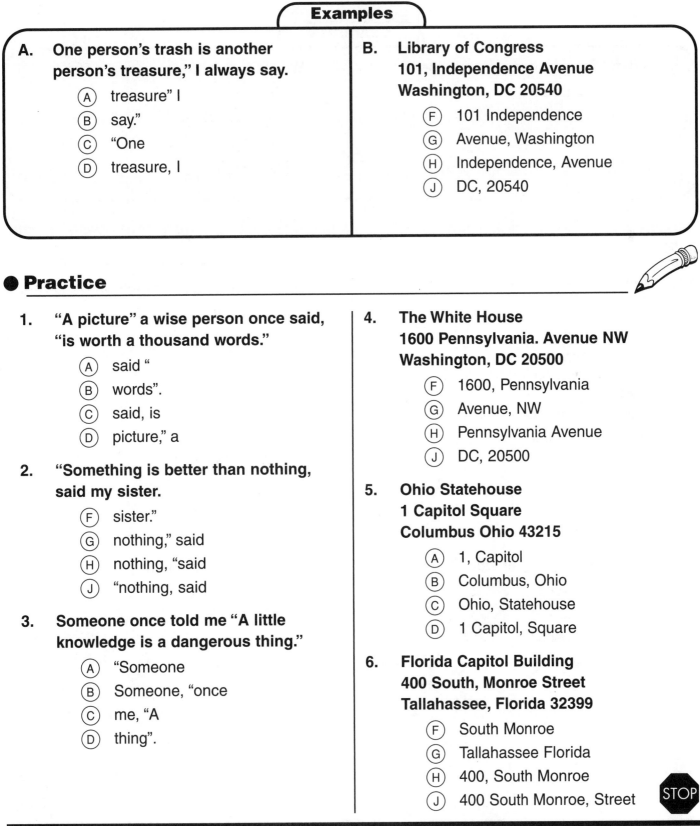

1. "A picture" a wise person once said, "is worth a thousand words."
   - Ⓐ said "
   - Ⓑ words".
   - Ⓒ said, is
   - Ⓓ picture," a

2. "Something is better than nothing, said my sister.
   - Ⓕ sister."
   - Ⓖ nothing," said
   - Ⓗ nothing, "said
   - Ⓙ "nothing, said

3. Someone once told me "A little knowledge is a dangerous thing."
   - Ⓐ "Someone
   - Ⓑ Someone, "once
   - Ⓒ me, "A
   - Ⓓ thing".

4. The White House
   1600 Pennsylvania. Avenue NW
   Washington, DC 20500
   - Ⓕ 1600, Pennsylvania
   - Ⓖ Avenue, NW
   - Ⓗ Pennsylvania Avenue
   - Ⓙ DC, 20500

5. Ohio Statehouse
   1 Capitol Square
   Columbus Ohio 43215
   - Ⓐ 1, Capitol
   - Ⓑ Columbus, Ohio
   - Ⓒ Ohio, Statehouse
   - Ⓓ 1 Capitol, Square

6. Florida Capitol Building
   400 South, Monroe Street
   Tallahassee, Florida 32399
   - Ⓕ South Monroe
   - Ⓖ Tallahassee Florida
   - Ⓗ 400, South Monroe
   - Ⓙ 400 South Monroe, Street

STOP

LANGUAGE: LANGUAGE MECHANICS

● Lesson 5: Possessives

Directions: Choose the correct word to complete each sentence.

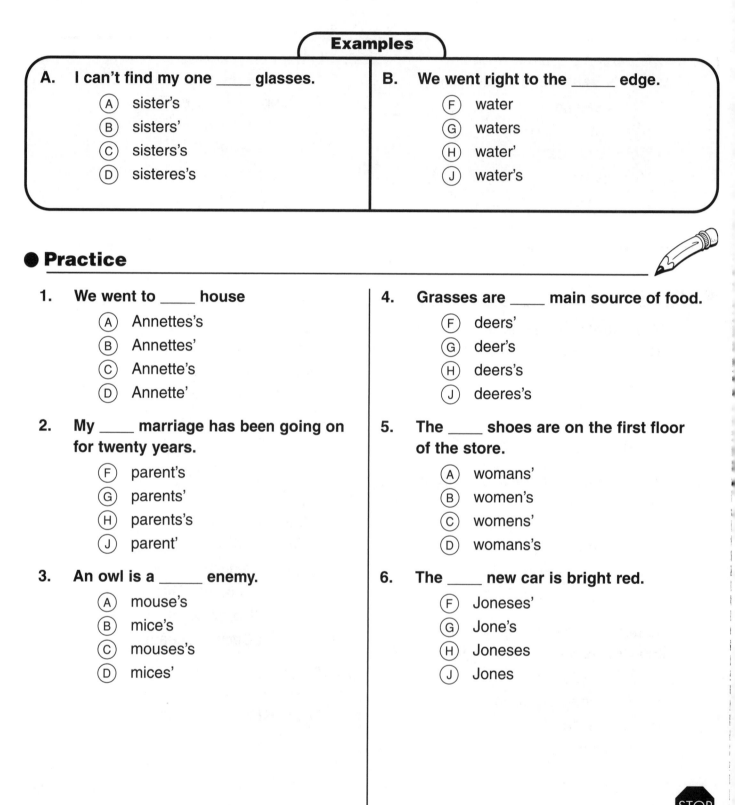

Examples

A. I can't find my one ____ glasses.
- (A) sister's
- (B) sisters'
- (C) sisters's
- (D) sisteres's

B. We went right to the _____ edge.
- (F) water
- (G) waters
- (H) water'
- (J) water's

● Practice

1. We went to ____ house
   - (A) Annettes's
   - (B) Annettes'
   - (C) Annette's
   - (D) Annette'

2. My ____ marriage has been going on for twenty years.
   - (F) parent's
   - (G) parents'
   - (H) parents's
   - (J) parent'

3. An owl is a _____ enemy.
   - (A) mouse's
   - (B) mice's
   - (C) mouses's
   - (D) mices'

4. Grasses are ____ main source of food.
   - (F) deers'
   - (G) deer's
   - (H) deers's
   - (J) deeres's

5. The ____ shoes are on the first floor of the store.
   - (A) womans'
   - (B) women's
   - (C) womens'
   - (D) womans's

6. The ____ new car is bright red.
   - (F) Joneses'
   - (G) Jone's
   - (H) Joneses
   - (J) Jones

STOP

LANGUAGE: LANGUAGE MECHANICS
SAMPLE TEST

Examples

For item A, choose the answer that shows a capital letter that is missing. If no capital letters are missing, choose the answer "None."

A.
- (A) I want
- (B) to read
- (C) *The Light in the window.*
- (D) None

For item B, choose the answer that shows the correct capitalization.

B. The ruler of England at that time was _____.
- (F) king George I
- (G) King George I
- (H) king george I
- (J) King George i

For numbers 1–3, choose the answer that shows a capital letter that is missing. If no capital letters are missing, choose the answer "None."

1.
- (A) Oliver knows
- (B) he isn't
- (C) supposed to do that.
- (D) None

2.
- (F) The theater
- (G) is on
- (H) Front street.
- (J) None

3.
- (A) did you
- (B) find your gift
- (C) on the table?
- (D) None

For numbers 4–5, choose the answer that shows the correct capitalization.

4. How was your visit with _____?
- (F) aunt alice
- (G) Aunt alice
- (H) Aunt Alice
- (J) aunt Alice

5. My uncle lives in _____.
- (A) Paris, france
- (B) paris, france
- (C) Paris, France
- (D) paris, France

GO ON

LANGUAGE: LANGUAGE MECHANICS
SAMPLE TEST (cont.)

For numbers 6–10, choose the answer that shows the correct punctuation mark. If no punctuation is missing, choose the answer "None."

6. **We have lots of birds in our backyard.**

   Ⓕ .
   Ⓖ ,
   Ⓗ !
   Ⓙ None

7. **Ms Wheatley is my sister's teacher.**

   Ⓐ .
   Ⓑ ?
   Ⓒ !
   Ⓓ None

8. **Hurry We're going to miss the bus!**

   Ⓕ .
   Ⓖ ?
   Ⓗ !
   Ⓙ None

9. **How many boxes of cookies did you sell**

   Ⓐ .
   Ⓑ ?
   Ⓒ !
   Ⓓ None

10. **We used to live in Detroit Michigan.**

    Ⓕ ,
    Ⓖ .
    Ⓗ !
    Ⓙ None

For numbers 11–14, choose the answer that shows the correct punctuation.

11. **The book _____ on the shelf.**

    Ⓐ wasn't
    Ⓑ wasnt
    Ⓒ was'nt
    Ⓓ wasn't'

12. **_____ forget to bring home your uniform!**

    Ⓕ Dont
    Ⓖ Don't
    Ⓗ Dont'
    Ⓙ Do'nt

13. **_____ a great friend.**

    Ⓐ Youre
    Ⓑ Your'e
    Ⓒ Youre'
    Ⓓ You're

14. **_____ great to be going on vacation!**

    Ⓕ Its
    Ⓖ I'ts
    Ⓗ Its'
    Ⓙ It's

GO ON

Name _____   Date_____

For numbers 15–20, choose the answer that shows the correct punctuation and capitalization.

15. Ⓐ The bus comes for us at 7:30
     Ⓑ terri likes to ride up front.
     Ⓒ My friends and I like to sit in the back.
     Ⓓ We talk about sports and TV shows?

16. Ⓕ On saturday mornings, we sleep in.
     Ⓖ dad makes pancakes.
     Ⓗ Then we all work on our chores.
     Ⓙ At the end of the day, We rent a movie to watch.

17. Ⓐ Yesterday, i got a new kitten!
     Ⓑ I have named her tara.
     Ⓒ She came from the animal shelter
     Ⓓ She has green eyes and black fur.

18. Ⓕ the house was dark and still.
     Ⓖ Suddenly, the door creaked open!
     Ⓗ Someone inside the house laughed
     Ⓙ It was my friend, michelle, playing a trick?

19. Ⓐ What is your favorite team?
     Ⓑ my dad likes the yankees.
     Ⓒ I always cheer for the red Sox.
     Ⓓ I cant believe you like the Tigers!

20. Ⓕ She and i will study now.
     Ⓖ the library is closed.
     Ⓗ Let's leave now?
     Ⓙ Can I borrow that book when you're done?

For numbers 21–23, read the passage. Then choose the answer that shows the correct capitalization and punctuation for the underlined phrase. Choose "Correct as it is" if the underlined part of the sentence is correct.

   lena lopez is my best friend. She gave me a great birthday gift. She bought both of us tickets to Bigtop amusement Park. We decided to go on Saturday, May 15, after our gymnastics class. We didn't want to go on the rides first, so we played some games. I won a teddy bear. Then we ate some cotton candy. We saved the rollercoaster for last!

21. Ⓐ Lena lopez is my Best Friend.
     Ⓑ Lena Lopez is my best friend.
     Ⓒ Lena Lopez is my Best friend.
     Ⓓ Correct as it is

22. Ⓕ Bigtop amusement park
     Ⓖ bigtop amusement park
     Ⓗ Bigtop Amusement Park
     Ⓙ Correct as it is

23. Ⓐ Saturday May 15,
     Ⓑ saturday, May 15
     Ⓒ Saturday, may, 15
     Ⓓ Correct as it is

LANGUAGE: LANGUAGE EXPRESSION

● Lesson 6: Nouns and Pronouns

Examples

Read each item. For A and numbers 1–3, choose the answer that completes the sentence best.

A. _____ love to dance.

- (A) He
- (B) She
- (C) They
- (D) Them

For B and numbers 4–6, choose the answer that could replace the underlined word.

B. Juan built a model rocket.

- (F) Him
- (G) He
- (H) Them
- (J) We

Clue If a question seems too hard, skip it and come back to it later.

● Practice

1. Fred and Janna gave _____ report today.
   - (A) him
   - (B) she
   - (C) them
   - (D) their

2. Please tell _____ to take this note home.
   - (F) she
   - (G) he
   - (H) her
   - (J) it

3. _____ called my father on Sunday.
   - (A) Him
   - (B) He
   - (C) Us
   - (D) Them

4. Tim and Lee washed the dishes.
   - (F) Him
   - (G) Them
   - (H) They
   - (J) She

5. Did Amanda get her computer repaired?
   - (A) her
   - (B) she
   - (C) it
   - (D) us

6. When did you notice the book was missing?
   - (F) him
   - (G) her
   - (H) we
   - (J) it

GO ON

Name _____ Date_____

LANGUAGE: LANGUAGE EXPRESSION

● **Lesson 6: Nouns and Pronouns (cont.)**

Examples

Read each item. For C and numbers 7–9, choose the answer that has a mistake.

C.
- (A) Do you think them will go shopping?
- (B) He doesn't like to eat red meat.
- (C) His father is going with him.
- (D) They will be back soon.

For D and numbers 10–12, choose the answer that has the simple subject of the sentence underlined.

D.
- (F) The black bear paced in his cage.
- (G) He seemed unhappy.
- (H) The noisy children watched him.
- (J) Some people like zoos.

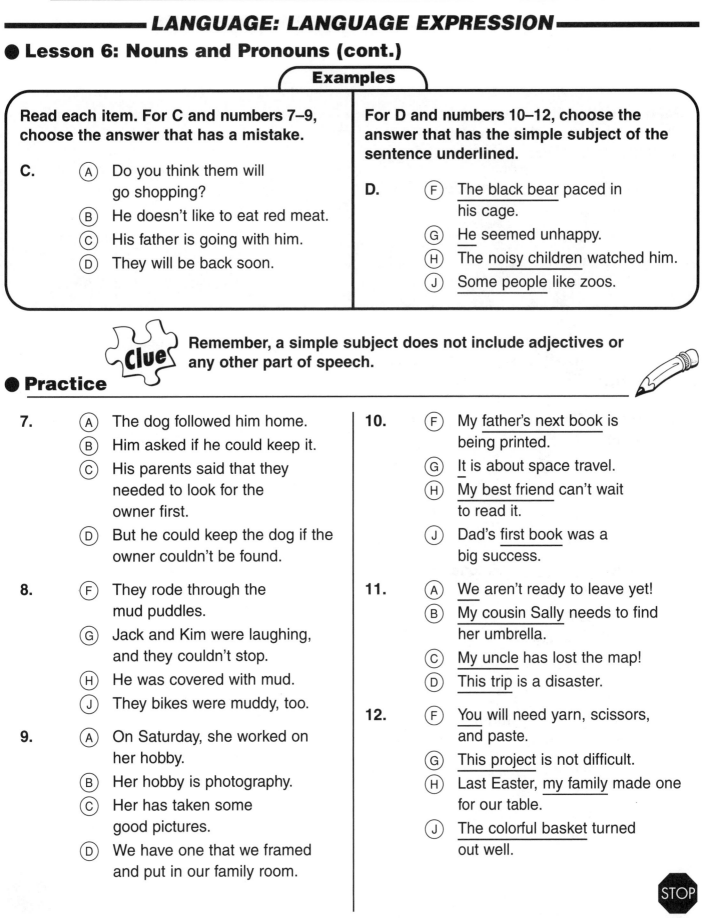

Clue Remember, a simple subject does not include adjectives or any other part of speech.

● **Practice**

7.
- (A) The dog followed him home.
- (B) Him asked if he could keep it.
- (C) His parents said that they needed to look for the owner first.
- (D) But he could keep the dog if the owner couldn't be found.

8.
- (F) They rode through the mud puddles.
- (G) Jack and Kim were laughing, and they couldn't stop.
- (H) He was covered with mud.
- (J) They bikes were muddy, too.

9.
- (A) On Saturday, she worked on her hobby.
- (B) Her hobby is photography.
- (C) Her has taken some good pictures.
- (D) We have one that we framed and put in our family room.

10.
- (F) My father's next book is being printed.
- (G) It is about space travel.
- (H) My best friend can't wait to read it.
- (J) Dad's first book was a big success.

11.
- (A) We aren't ready to leave yet!
- (B) My cousin Sally needs to find her umbrella.
- (C) My uncle has lost the map!
- (D) This trip is a disaster.

12.
- (F) You will need yarn, scissors, and paste.
- (G) This project is not difficult.
- (H) Last Easter, my family made one for our table.
- (J) The colorful basket turned out well.

STOP

LANGUAGE: LANGUAGE EXPRESSION

● Lesson 7: Verbs

Examples

Read each item. For A and numbers 1–3, choose the answer that completes the sentence best.

A. The gift _____ yesterday.

- (A) arrives
- (B) arrived
- (C) arriving
- (D) will arrive

For B and numbers 4–6, choose the answer that uses an incorrect verb.

B.
- (F) The library have a room for music.
- (G) In the room, you can listen to recordings.
- (H) The room has lots of books about music.
- (J) I love spending time there.

Clue If you aren't sure which answer is correct, read each choice softly to yourself.

● Practice

1. Jeff and Channa _____ us make bread.
- (A) had help
- (B) will help
- (C) helps
- (D) helping

2. Please _____ this letter to the post office.
- (F) took
- (G) has taken
- (H) tooked
- (J) take

3. No one _____ him about the change of plans.
- (A) telled
- (B) told
- (C) tells
- (D) did tell

4.
- (F) Chang has pick up her heavy backpack.
- (G) She carries that backpack everywhere.
- (H) It has all her art supplies in it.
- (J) She also carries her laptop in the backpack.

5.
- (A) He forgot to take his jacket home.
- (B) It were a cold day.
- (C) He shivered without his jacket.
- (D) He was very glad to get home at last.

6.
- (F) Nobody is home today.
- (G) The house is locked up.
- (H) It look strange with the shades down.
- (J) I am not used to seeing it so empty.

STOP

⎯⎯⎯⎯⎯⎯ *LANGUAGE: LANGUAGE EXPRESSION* ⎯⎯⎯⎯⎯⎯

● **Lesson 8: Adjectives**

┌─────────────── **Examples** ───────────────┐

Read each item. For A and numbers 1–3, choose the word or phrase that completes the sentence best.

A. That is the _____ ice cream I've ever had.

- Ⓐ better
- Ⓑ most best
- Ⓒ best
- Ⓓ good

For B and numbers 4–6, choose the sentence that is written correctly.

B.
- Ⓕ It was the most small elephant.
- Ⓖ First, she climbed onto the tallest platform.
- Ⓗ Then the most short clown climbed up, too.
- Ⓙ These greater circus performers danced together.

Clue If you are sure that you know the right answer, mark it and move right on to the next question.

● **Practice**

1. **Albert is the _____ person I know.**
   - Ⓐ funny
   - Ⓑ more funny
   - Ⓒ funnier
   - Ⓓ funniest

2. **I think my new dog is the _____ birthday present I've ever had.**
   - Ⓕ most wonderful
   - Ⓖ wonderfullest
   - Ⓗ more wonderful
   - Ⓙ wonderful

3. **I would like the _____ of the two pieces of cake.**
   - Ⓐ smallest
   - Ⓑ small
   - Ⓒ smaller
   - Ⓓ more small

4.
   - Ⓕ I think camping is the funnest thing to do.
   - Ⓖ We take our biggest tent, the one with the little window.
   - Ⓗ We find the more quiet campsite we can.
   - Ⓙ I think our favoriter place is by a little lake in the woods.

5.
   - Ⓐ This is my most better coat.
   - Ⓑ It is the brightest red that I've ever seen.
   - Ⓒ It is also more warmer than my other coats.
   - Ⓓ This more good coat is my favorite.

6.
   - Ⓕ The more emptier house is up for sale.
   - Ⓖ My most best friend used to live there.
   - Ⓗ Her mother is the kindest person I know.
   - Ⓙ I was so saddest to see them move away.

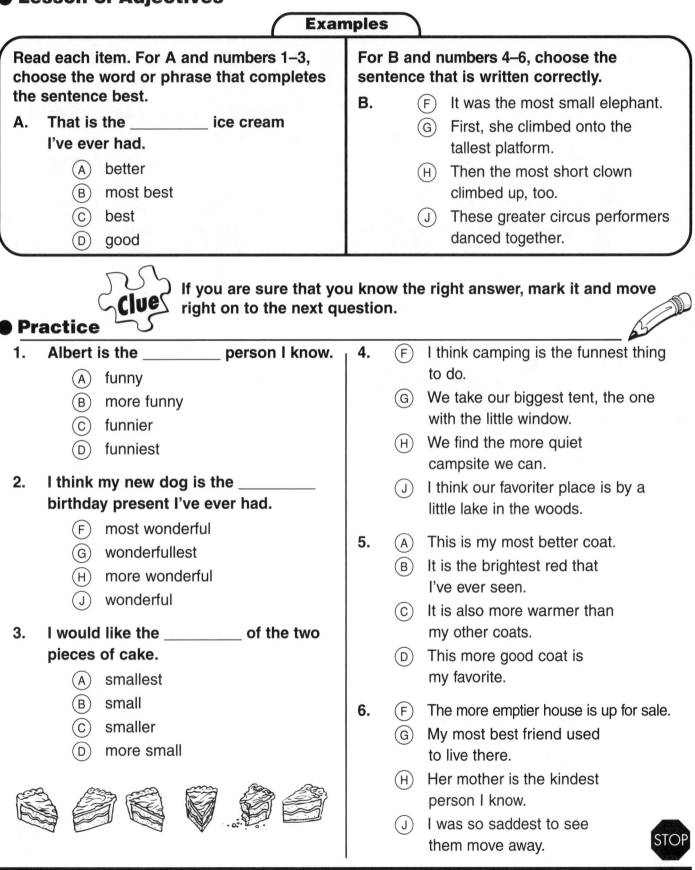

STOP

LANGUAGE: LANGUAGE EXPRESSION

● Lesson 9: Sentences

Examples

Read each item. For A and numbers 1–5, choose the sentence that is written correctly.

A.
   Ⓐ Mr. Woo opens his store early.
   Ⓑ Always kind to us.
   Ⓒ Food and other things.
   Ⓓ Like to shop there.

For B and numbers 6–10, choose the best combination of the underlined sentences.

B.   <u>It rained like cats and dogs.</u> <u>It rained all night long.</u>
   Ⓕ Like cats and dogs, it rained all night long.
   Ⓖ It rained all night long, and like cats and dogs.
   Ⓗ It rained like cats and dogs and it rained all night long.
   Ⓙ It rained like cats and dogs all night long.

Clue   Read the choices carefully to yourself. Choose the one that sounds correct.

● Practice

1.
   Ⓐ We are going on a trip.
   Ⓑ To Japan, China, and Korea.
   Ⓒ Packing our suitcases.
   Ⓓ Can't wait to travel and have fun!

2.
   Ⓕ Jars of paint are out.
   Ⓖ Painting of trees and flowers.
   Ⓗ I am going to paint for an hour.
   Ⓙ Wonderful to have art class.

3.
   Ⓐ The American flag.
   Ⓑ Red, white, and blue.
   Ⓒ Thirteen stripes, one for each colony.
   Ⓓ Our flag today has 50 stars.

4.
   Ⓕ Caleb finished lunch at one o'clock.
   Ⓖ Chicken sandwich, juice, and an apple.
   Ⓗ All packed in a brown paper bag.
   Ⓙ Caleb's lunch hour over.

5.
   Ⓐ The train is coming down the tracks.
   Ⓑ Can hear the rumbling of the train.
   Ⓒ A bright headlight and a loud whistle.
   Ⓓ Fifty cars and a caboose.

GO ON

LANGUAGE: LANGUAGE EXPRESSION

● Lesson 9: Sentences (cont.)

For numbers 6–10, choose the best combination of the underlined sentences.

6. **Field Day is my favorite day at school.**
   Field Day is May 10.
   - (F) Field Day is my favorite day at school and it is May 10.
   - (G) Field Day, my favorite day at school, is May 10.
   - (H) Field Day is May 10, my favorite day at school.
   - (J) Field Day is my favorite day, May 10, at school.

7. **I like pizza for dinner.**
   I like mushroom pizza.
   - (A) I like mushroom pizza, and I like it for dinner.
   - (B) I like pizza, mushroom pizza, for dinner.
   - (C) I like mushroom pizza for dinner.
   - (D) I like pizza for dinner, and I like mushroom pizza.

8. **Parrots live in the tropics.**
   Parrots are beautiful birds.
   - (F) Parrots are beautiful birds that live in the tropics.
   - (G) Parrots, beautiful birds, live in the tropics.
   - (H) Parrots live in the tropics and are beautiful birds.
   - (J) Parrots, that live in the tropics, are beautiful birds.

9. **The trees are in the forest.**
   The trees are tall.
   - (A) The trees are in the forest, and are tall.
   - (B) The tall trees, they are in the forest.
   - (C) The trees in the forest are tall.
   - (D) The trees, tall, are in the forest.

10. **The birds come to the feeder.**
    The birds are red and blue.
    - (F) The red and blue birds come to the feeder.
    - (G) The birds, red and blue, come to the feeder.
    - (H) The birds are red and blue, and they come to the feeder.
    - (J) The birds come to the feeder, red and blue.

GO ON

Name _____   Date_____

● **Lesson 9: Sentences (cont.)**

Read the letter. Then answer numbers 11–14 about the letter. If the sentence needs no changes, choose "Correct as it is."

Dear Ms. Wood:

   (1) Our whole class would like to thank you for the nature trail tour. **(2)** We was amazed at the number of flowers, and animals, on the trail. **(3)** The birds and animals, all of them that we saw, were so beautiful. **(4)** We drew pictures of some of the birds and animals after we got back to school. **(5)** The wildflowers, which we saw on the nature trail, were colorful and interesting. **(6)** Our favorite was the one called Queen Anne's lace. **(7)** We are sending you a drawing of this flower as a thank-you for the tour.

Sincerely,

Mrs. Jasper's Third Grade Class

11.   Sentence 2 is best written—

Ⓐ   We were amazed by the number of flowers, and animals, on the trail.

Ⓑ   The flowers and animals was amazing on the trail.

Ⓒ   We were amazed at the number of flowers and animals on the trail.

Ⓓ   Correct as it is

12.   Sentence 3 is best written—

Ⓕ   The birds and animals that we seen were so beautiful.

Ⓖ   All of the birds and animals that we saw were so beautiful.

Ⓗ   All of the birds and all of the animals we saw were so beautiful.

Ⓙ   Correct as it is

13.   Sentence 5 is best written—

Ⓐ   The wildflowers that we saw on the nature trail were colorful and interesting.

Ⓑ   We saw on the trail wildflowers which were colorful and interesting.

Ⓒ   Wildflowers, colorful and interesting, which we saw on the trail.

Ⓓ   Correct as it is

14.   Sentence 7 is best written—

Ⓕ   We are sending you this flower, a drawing, as a thank-you for the tour.

Ⓖ   As a thank-you, we are sending you this drawing, of this flower.

Ⓗ   Thank-you for the tour, we are sending you this drawing of a flower.

Ⓙ   Correct as it is

LANGUAGE: LANGUAGE EXPRESSION

● Lesson 10: Paragraphs

Directions: Read each paragraph. Choose the answer that best fills in the blank as the topic sentence of the paragraph.

Example

A. _____. After President John Adams moved in, the outside was painted white. However, the name *White House* did not come into use until much later, when President Theodore Roosevelt had the name put on his writing paper.

- (A) The President's house was not always known as the White House.
- (B) George Washington did not want to live in the White House.
- (C) The White House was burned down during the War of 1812.
- (D) President Roosevelt, who lived in the White House, loved to ride horses.

Clue Remember, a paragraph should contain one idea. All of the sentences should relate to that idea.

● Practice

1. _____. Some sand looks white and seems to sparkle. Some sand may be light tan, black, or even pink. Sand has the same color as the rocks from which it was made. Looking at sand under a magnifying glass makes it possible to see the sparkling colors more clearly.

- (A) Sand can be made up of large or small grains.
- (B) All sand looks about the same.
- (C) Not all sand looks the same.
- (D) The color of sand is very important.

2. _____. They help keep bits of dust from getting into our eyes. They act as umbrellas, keeping the rain from our eyes. They also help shade our eyes from the sun. Like the frame around a beautiful painting, eyelashes play an important part in keeping our eyes safe.

- (F) Eyelashes can be blonde, brown, or black.
- (G) Eyelashes protect our eyes from harm.
- (H) Do you have long eyelashes?
- (J) Eyelashes can be straight or curled.

GO ON

LANGUAGE: LANGUAGE EXPRESSION

● Lesson 10: Paragraphs (cont.)

For numbers 3–4, read the topic sentence. Then choose the answer that develops the topic sentence in the best way.

3. **The canary is one of the best-liked of all pet birds.**

   (A) Canaries are not only pretty, but they sing cheerful songs.

   (B) Canaries can be yellow, red, or orange.

   (C) You have to be careful with a pet bird, or it may escape.

   (D) Canaries like to live in the Canary Islands.

4. **Some animals and insects are speedy creatures.**

   (F) A hummingbird can fly 60 miles an hour, and a duck can fly twice that fast.

   (G) Snails move very slowly.

   (H) Ducks and hummingbirds are both birds.

   (J) There are animals that are fast and some that are slow.

For numbers 5–7, read the paragraph. Then answer the questions.

(1) These people face some difficulties in looking at the world around them. (2) To the color blind, for example, red and green look like the same colors. (3) A color-blind person might have trouble telling a ripe tomato from an unripe one. (4) There are also some people in the world who cannot see any colors. (5) To them, everything looks black, white, or gray.

5. **Choose the best topic sentence for this paragraph.**

   (A) People who cannot tell one color from another are said to be *color blind*.

   (B) To these people, yellow and brown are the main colors they can see.

   (C) A color-blind person cannot see any colors.

   (D) Red and green are hard to tell apart.

6. **Choose the best last sentence for this paragraph.**

   (F) Color blindness can make some tasks difficult.

   (G) Color blindness creates special challenges, but does not keep people from leading normal lives.

   (H) People with color blindness look like other people.

   (J) Some animals are color blind, too.

7. **Choose the best sentence to add between Sentences 3 and 4.**

   (A) These people might also have difficulty telling "stop" from "go" on a traffic light.

   (B) Color blindness can be measured with special tests.

   (C) Color-blind people do not look different from other people.

   (D) Color blindness may be cured in the future with special glasses.

   GO ON ➡

LANGUAGE: LANGUAGE EXPRESSION

● **Lesson 10: Paragraphs (cont.)**

Read the essay. Then answer questions 8–11.

(1) Put about four spoonfuls of water and one spoonful of sugar in a very small, open bottle. (2) Paint the bottle red. (3) Then hang the bottle under an overhanging roof or near a window. (4) If you plant red flowers, they will help, too. (5) The tiny hummingbirds will come to drink the sugar water. (6) The hummingbird will think that the bright feeder is another flower, and the sugar water is flower nectar. (7) Hummingbirds like brightly colored flowers that have lots of nectar.

8. **Choose the best topic sentence for this paragraph.**

   Ⓕ Here's how to attract hummingbirds to your backyard.

   Ⓖ Hummingbirds are among the fastest flyers in the bird world.

   Ⓗ Do you like hummingbirds?

   Ⓙ Hummingbirds are colorful birds.

9. **Choose a sentence to take out of the essay.**

   Ⓐ Sentence 1

   Ⓑ Sentence 3

   Ⓒ Sentence 4

   Ⓓ Sentence 6

10. **Choose a better place for Sentence 7.**

    Ⓕ Between Sentence 1 and Sentence 2

    Ⓖ Between Sentence 2 and Sentence 3

    Ⓗ Between Sentence 3 and Sentence 4

    Ⓙ Between Sentence 5 and Sentence 6

11. **Choose the best sentence to add to the end of the essay.**

    Ⓐ Hummingbirds are as brightly colored as the flowers they like best.

    Ⓑ Hummingbirds are fast flyers and dart from place to place.

    Ⓒ By building a simple feeder, you can help hummingbirds and enjoy them in your yard.

    Ⓓ By building a simple feeder, you can trick hummingbirds.

STOP

LANGUAGE: LANGUAGE EXPRESSION
SAMPLE TEST

Examples

Read each item. For A, choose the answer that completes the sentence best.

A. _____ likes to bake cookies.
- (A) He
- (B) Us
- (C) They
- (D) Them

For B, choose the answer that could replace the underlined word.

B. **Tyrone** has a baseball card collection.
- (F) Him
- (G) He
- (H) We
- (J) Them

For numbers 1–3, choose the answer that completes the sentence best.

1. **Chang and Audrey made _____ kites together.**
   - (A) him
   - (B) she
   - (C) them
   - (D) their

2. **Are _____ parents coming to the concert?**
   - (F) she
   - (G) he
   - (H) her
   - (J) it

3. **_____ spoke to my mother on Parents' Night.**
   - (A) Him
   - (B) He
   - (C) Us
   - (D) Them

For numbers 4–6, choose the answer that could replace the underlined word.

4. **Jill and Keisha went to soccer practice.**
   - (F) Him
   - (G) Them
   - (H) They
   - (J) She

5. **Did Brian find his lost cat?**
   - (A) him
   - (B) he
   - (C) it
   - (D) us

6. **I thought the play was very good.**
   - (F) him
   - (G) her
   - (H) we
   - (J) it

GO ON

LANGUAGE: LANGUAGE EXPRESSION
SAMPLE TEST (cont.)

Read each item. For numbers 7–12, choose the answer that completes the sentence best.

7. Ms. Bentley _____ us with the math lesson.

- Ⓐ don't help
- Ⓑ will help
- Ⓒ would helping
- Ⓓ helping

8. Please _____ the band uniform tomorrow.

- Ⓕ buy
- Ⓖ buyed
- Ⓗ bought
- Ⓙ boughten

9. Kara _____ us about her trip to Scotland yesterday.

- Ⓐ telled
- Ⓑ told
- Ⓒ tells
- Ⓓ did told

10. He _____ the windows carefully.

- Ⓕ wipe
- Ⓖ did wiping
- Ⓗ wiping
- Ⓙ wiped

11. The music _____ from the car.

- Ⓐ blasted
- Ⓑ blast
- Ⓒ had blast
- Ⓓ blasting

12. Latoya _____ to hike with her family.

- Ⓕ did liked
- Ⓖ liking
- Ⓗ likes
- Ⓙ like

For numbers 13–16, choose the answer that uses an incorrect verb.

13.
- Ⓐ The skipper steering the boat.
- Ⓑ The wind blew across the lake.
- Ⓒ The boat stayed on course.
- Ⓓ The brave skipper brought the boat safely to shore.

14.
- Ⓕ The dentist cleaned my teeth.
- Ⓖ I was worried he might have to use the drill.
- Ⓗ He were very nice.
- Ⓙ My teeth are shiny now!

15.
- Ⓐ The pioneer chose his land carefully.
- Ⓑ He wanted a stream near his cabin.
- Ⓒ He wanting good land for crops.
- Ⓓ He knew he could use the trees for building.

16.
- Ⓕ Who wants to go with me to the game?
- Ⓖ My sister is a good basketball player.
- Ⓗ Her team is in first place.
- Ⓙ I would cheering for her team to win.

GO ON

LANGUAGE: LANGUAGE EXPRESSION
SAMPLE TEST (cont.)

Read each item. For numbers 17–20, choose the word or phrase that completes the sentence best.

17. **Amelia is the _____ person I have met.**
    - (A) sincere
    - (B) sincerer
    - (C) more sincere
    - (D) most sincere

18. **I think that the _____ puppy will get tired first.**
    - (F) most energetic
    - (G) energetic
    - (H) energeticer
    - (J) energeticest

19. **Please give me the _____ doll on the shelf.**
    - (A) largest
    - (B) more large
    - (C) most large
    - (D) larger

20. **The parade will be _____ if you bring a chair.**
    - (F) enjoyablest
    - (G) most enjoyabler
    - (H) more enjoyable
    - (J) enjoyabler

For numbers 21–24, choose the sentence that is written correctly.

21.
   - (A) Mice are biggest eaters.
   - (B) They will eat soap or paper if they can't find food.
   - (C) Mice are littler, but they eat all of the time.
   - (D) Mice are not pickiest eaters.

22.
   - (F) Some of the most small insects lay tiny eggs.
   - (G) Housefly eggs are bigger than the eggs of most insects.
   - (H) Twenty-five of these biggest eggs fit into one inch.
   - (J) There are largest eggs than those of the housefly.

23.
   - (A) Fill the more small bottle with water.
   - (B) Then add some of the heavy cooking oil.
   - (C) Be sure to put on the yellower cap before your shake the bottle!
   - (D) Oil and water do not mix good.

24.
   - (F) Jim's hair was the longer it had ever been.
   - (G) He walked slow to the barber shop.
   - (H) The barber cut Jim's hair very shorter.
   - (J) Jim likes his shorter hair now.

GO ON

LANGUAGE: LANGUAGE EXPRESSION
SAMPLE TEST (cont.)

Read the journal entry. Then answer numbers 25–29 about the entry. If the sentence needs no changes, choose "Correct as it is."

(1) My parents and I, we are flying to Chicago tomorrow. (2) My father is attending a business conference. (3) While Dad is working, Mom and I am seeing the sights (4) Go to the top of the Hancock Building and the Willis Tower. (5) We will visiting my Aunt Ruth, too. (6) I can hardly wait to go! (7) We were leaving at seven o'clock tomorrow morning.

25. **Sentence 1 is best written—**
   (A) My parents and I are flying to Chicago tomorrow.
   (B) My parents and I were flying to Chicago tomorrow.
   (C) My parents and I, we flew to Chicago tomorrow.
   (D) Correct as it is

26. **Sentence 2 is best written—**
   (F) My father is attended a business conference.
   (G) My father will attending a business conference.
   (H) My father attends a business conference.
   (J) Correct as it is

27. **Sentence 3 is best written—**
   (A) While Dad working, Mom and I will see the sights.
   (B) While Dad is working, Mom and I will see the sights.
   (C) While Dad is working, Mom and I are seen the sights.
   (D) Correct as it is

28. **Sentence 5 is best written—**
   (F) We have visited my Aunt Ruth, too.
   (G) We will be visiting my Aunt Ruth, too.
   (H) We are visit my Aunt Ruth, too.
   (J) Correct as it is

29. **Which of these is not a sentence?**
   (A) Sentence 1
   (B) Sentence 3
   (C) Sentence 4
   (D) Sentence 7

GO ON

LANGUAGE: LANGUAGE EXPRESSION
SAMPLE TEST (cont.)

Read each item. For numbers 30–33, choose the sentence that is written correctly.

30.
- (F) Them cookies we baked are terrible.
- (G) Even the dog won't eat them.
- (H) When I dropping one, it made a loud noise.
- (J) I are not sure that we can eat them.

31.
- (A) I could had done those problems.
- (B) Didn't need help.
- (C) I listened carefully in class.
- (D) I knowed how to do them.

32.
- (F) The campers watched in horror as the bear took their food.
- (G) Scrambled eggs, bacon, and juice.
- (H) The bear dranked all the juice last.
- (J) He did to like his breakfast that morning.

33.
- (A) Concert in the park last night.
- (B) Music, dancing, and cheering.
- (C) Over a thousand people was there.
- (D) I will never forget that concert.

For numbers 34–36, choose the best combination of the underlined sentences.

34. Jack is late.
    Jack has gotten lost.
- (F) Jack is late and Jack has gotten lost.
- (G) Jack has gotten lost and he is late.
- (H) Jack, gotten lost, is late.
- (J) Jack, is late, and has gotten lost.

35. Jody is my best friend.
    Jody is my cousin.
- (A) My best friend, Jody is my cousin.
- (B) My cousin Jody, Jody is my best friend.
- (C) My cousin Jody is my best friend.
- (D) My best friend and cousin is Jody.

36. Maggie is visiting her grandmother.
    Maggie's grandmother lives in Arizona.
- (F) In Arizona, Maggie is visiting her grandmother.
- (G) Maggie is visiting Arizona and her grandmother.
- (H) Maggie's grandmother is being visited by Maggie in Arizona.
- (J) Maggie is visiting her grandmother in Arizona.

GO ON

LANGUAGE: LANGUAGE EXPRESSION
SAMPLE TEST (cont.)

For numbers 37–39, read the paragraph. Then choose the answer that is the best topic sentence for the paragraph.

37. _____. **First, I think it would be fun to spend time with my friends. Second, we have not had a homemade cake in a long time. Third, my sister and brother would enjoy a birthday party, too.**

(A) I would like to invite six friends.

(B) I am turning nine in two weeks.

(C) I would like a new computer game for my birthday.

(D) I think I should be able to have a birthday party for three reasons.

38. _____. **Winter is white with snow. The cold air feels good on my face. I love building forts and making snow angels. I also love drinking hot chocolate in front of the fire.**

(F) Winter is my favorite season.

(G) In winter, you can go ice skating.

(H) In some places, it doesn't snow in the winter.

(J) I don't like winter.

39. _____. **Surfing and bike riding are her favorites, but she's good at lots of different sports. Trina won a championship in tennis, and she is also a good swimmer. In the winter, she likes to go skiing and skating.**

(A) Trina is a good baseball player.

(B) Trina is a good student.

(C) Trina loves sports.

(D) Trina won a swimming medal.

GO ON

Name _____ Date _____

For numbers 40–43, read the paragraph. Then answer the questions.

(1) When the rocks were brought back to Earth, people studied them. (2) Many things about the moon. (3) One discovery was the age of the moon. (4) The rocks also told us that there is very little water on the moon. (5) The moon is 4.2 billion years old.

40. Choose the best topic sentence for this paragraph.

- (F) In the 1960s, there was a race to get to the moon.
- (G) In 1969, three men landed on the moon.
- (H) Neil Armstrong was the first man to step onto the moon's surface.
- (J) In 1969, astronauts brought back rocks from the moon.

41. Choose the best last sentence for this paragraph.

- (A) The first journey to the moon helped us learn more about our universe.
- (B) The United States won the race to the moon.
- (C) I wonder what the astronauts thought about the moon?
- (D) The moon is very old.

42. Choose the best sentence to add between Sentences 3 and 4.

- (F) The rocks from space were looked at in a lab.
- (G) The moon rocks were very valuable.
- (H) By studying the moon rocks, we learned more about the moon's soil.
- (J) The astronauts kept some moon rocks for themselves.

43. Which choice is not a complete sentence?

- (A) Sentence 1
- (B) Sentence 2
- (C) Sentence 3
- (D) Sentence 4

LANGUAGE: SPELLING

● Lesson 11: Spelling

Examples

For A and numbers 1–3, choose the word that fits into the sentence and is spelled correctly.

A. She is not _____ to go.

- (A) eble
- (B) able
- (C) abel
- (D) abell

For B and numbers 4–6, choose the word that is spelled incorrectly. If all of the words are spelled correctly, choose "No mistakes."

B.
- (F) attack
- (G) funnel
- (H) cousin
- (J) No mistakes

Clue Read the directions carefully. In this lesson, you will be looking for both correctly and incorrectly spelled words.

● Practice

1. Please don't _____ your new shirt.
   - (A) winkle
   - (B) wrinkle
   - (C) wrinkel
   - (D) wrinekle

2. The _____ is surrounded with flowers.
   - (F) fountin
   - (G) fontain
   - (H) fountein
   - (J) fountain

3. Jane treated her book _____.
   - (A) carlessly
   - (B) carelessly
   - (C) carelesly
   - (D) carelissly

4.
   - (F) copper
   - (G) relaxing
   - (H) bandege
   - (J) No mistakes

5.
   - (A) foraign
   - (B) perfume
   - (C) tablet
   - (D) No mistakes

6.
   - (F) sunrise
   - (G) shephard
   - (H) furniture
   - (J) No mistakes

GO ON

● **Lesson 11: Spelling (cont.)**

For numbers 7–15, choose the word that is spelled incorrectly.

7.
   - (A) enjineer
   - (B) dryer
   - (C) mineral
   - (D) daisy

8.
   - (F) diary
   - (G) nationel
   - (H) pronoun
   - (J) barrel

9.
   - (A) period
   - (B) unusal
   - (C) president
   - (D) promise

10.
   - (F) curtain
   - (G) cryed
   - (H) morning
   - (J) bath

11.
   - (A) giant
   - (B) interesting
   - (C) trash
   - (D) thousend

12.
   - (F) biology
   - (G) vacation
   - (H) exemple
   - (J) absent

13.
   - (A) agree
   - (B) elbow
   - (C) wooden
   - (D) woolan

14.
   - (F) lonely
   - (G) fansy
   - (H) ferry
   - (J) bacon

15.
   - (A) continew
   - (B) carve
   - (C) deer
   - (D) hawk

For numbers 16–20, read each sentence. Look for the underlined word that is spelled incorrectly and choose that phrase. Choose "No mistakes" if the sentence is correct.

16.
   - (F) The two girls
   - (G) jumped into the pool
   - (H) with a huje splash.
   - (J) No mistakes

17.
   - (A) My favorite samwich
   - (B) is peanut butter
   - (C) and grape jelly.
   - (D) No mistakes

18.
   - (F) Pam's dollhouse
   - (G) has real lites
   - (H) and a staircase.
   - (J) No mistakes

19.
   - (A) Wolf pups
   - (B) play outdoors
   - (C) when they are three weeks old.
   - (D) No mistakes

20.
   - (F) Thick, black smoke
   - (G) poored out
   - (H) of all the windows.
   - (J) No mistakes

STOP

LANGUAGE: SPELLING

● Lesson 12: Spelling Regular and Irregular Plurals

Directions: Choose the correct plural form to complete each sentence.

Examples

A. I have two favorite _____.
- (A) pair of pants
- (B) pairs of pant
- (C) pairs of pants
- (D) pair of pant

B. They had four ___ before they won a game.
- (F) loss's
- (G) loss'es
- (H) loss
- (J) losses

● Practice

1. I hear the patter of little ____.
- (A) foots
- (B) feet
- (C) footes
- (D) feetes

2. Several _____ blew down in the storm.
- (F) branches
- (G) branchs
- (H) branch's
- (J) branches's

3. Five of the ____ came to the concert.
- (A) Bretzs
- (B) Bretzes
- (C) Bretz
- (D) Bretz's

4. I have two pairs of ____.
- (F) eyeglass
- (G) eyeglass's
- (H) eyeglasses
- (J) eyesglasses

5. Pass out all the ___.
- (A) scissors
- (B) scissor
- (C) scissor's
- (D) scissores

6. I have four _____.
- (F) brother's-in-law
- (G) brother-in-laws
- (H) brothers-in-laws
- (J) brothers-in-law

STOP

LANGUAGE: SPELLING
SAMPLE TEST

Examples

For A and numbers 1–4, choose the word that fits into the sentence and is spelled correctly.

A. He shot the _____ into the air.

- (A) arrow
- (B) errow
- (C) airrow
- (D) airow

For B and numbers 5–8, choose the word that is spelled incorrectly. If all of the words are spelled correctly, choose "No mistakes."

B.
- (F) toast
- (G) rooster
- (H) emeny
- (J) No mistakes

---

1. Kiko has a new _____.

- (A) wissel
- (B) whistill
- (C) whistle
- (D) wistle

2. Sabrina wouldn't _____ to do that!

- (F) dare
- (G) dair
- (H) daire
- (J) dere

3. The cord would not _____ that far.

- (A) strech
- (B) stretch
- (C) stretsh
- (D) streitch

4. Did you _____ your seatbelt?

- (F) fastin
- (G) fassen
- (H) fastain
- (J) fasten

5.
- (A) suffer
- (B) pleasure
- (C) pleasant
- (D) No mistakes

6.
- (F) imagene
- (G) marry
- (H) court
- (J) No mistakes

7.
- (A) toughest
- (B) principal
- (C) emergensy
- (D) No mistakes

8.
- (F) public
- (G) prepair
- (H) frown
- (J) No mistakes

GO ON

LANGUAGE: SPELLING
SAMPLE TEST (cont.)

For numbers 9–17, choose the word that is spelled correctly.

9.
- (A) beaf
- (B) cideer
- (C) cheif
- (D) miracle

10.
- (F) graduete
- (G) strayt
- (H) solar
- (J) calander

11.
- (A) mayor
- (B) honer
- (C) experiance
- (D) tuff

12.
- (F) enough
- (G) releese
- (H) foldar
- (J) decerate

13.
- (A) villaje
- (B) diskuss
- (C) contast
- (D) squirrel

14.
- (F) wherevar
- (G) prisaner
- (H) invitation
- (J) blendar

15.
- (A) babys
- (B) sneekers
- (C) progrem
- (D) product

16.
- (F) iland
- (G) melan
- (H) humid
- (J) dutys

17.
- (A) sprinkle
- (B) posishun
- (C) gymasium
- (D) billyan

For numbers 18–22, read each sentence. Look for the underlined word that is spelled incorrectly and choose that phrase. Choose "No mistakes" if the sentence is correct.

18.
- (F) The hidden passege
- (G) was flooded
- (H) with freezing water.
- (J) No mistakes

19.
- (A) The quiet village
- (B) was destroied
- (C) by the giant.
- (D) No mistakes

20.
- (F) The engine
- (G) had stopped
- (H) on the mountain.
- (J) No mistakes

21.
- (A) It seems a shame
- (B) to waist
- (C) such a beautiful day.
- (D) No mistakes

22.
- (F) In a foreign country,
- (G) you cannot expect
- (H) people to speak English.
- (J) No mistakes

STOP

LANGUAGE: STUDY SKILLS

● Lesson 13: Study Skills

Directions: Read each item. Choose the answer that you think is correct.

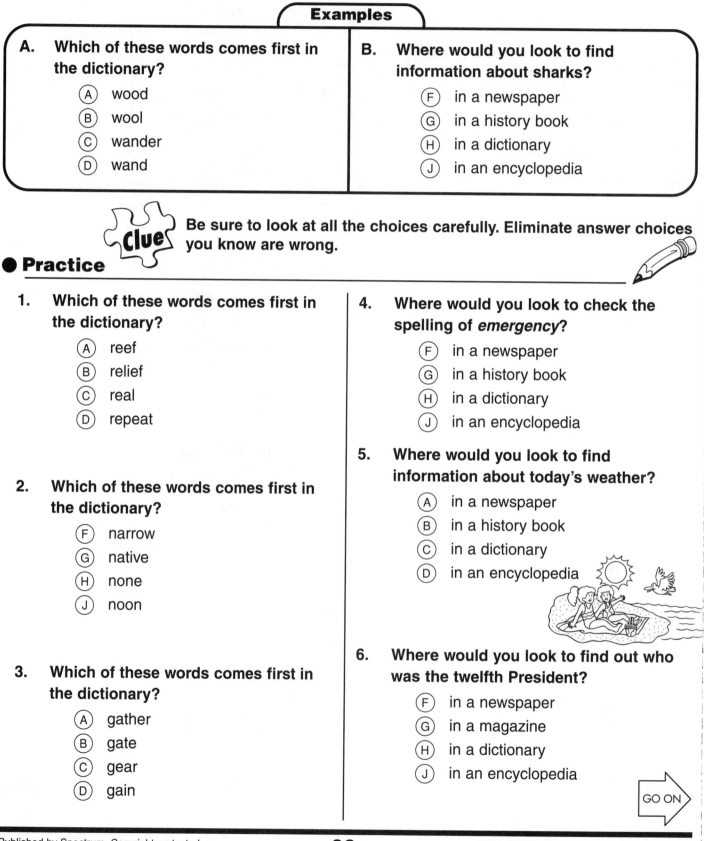

Examples

A. Which of these words comes first in the dictionary?

- (A) wood
- (B) wool
- (C) wander
- (D) wand

B. Where would you look to find information about sharks?

- (F) in a newspaper
- (G) in a history book
- (H) in a dictionary
- (J) in an encyclopedia

Clue Be sure to look at all the choices carefully. Eliminate answer choices you know are wrong.

● Practice

1. Which of these words comes first in the dictionary?

- (A) reef
- (B) relief
- (C) real
- (D) repeat

2. Which of these words comes first in the dictionary?

- (F) narrow
- (G) native
- (H) none
- (J) noon

3. Which of these words comes first in the dictionary?

- (A) gather
- (B) gate
- (C) gear
- (D) gain

4. Where would you look to check the spelling of *emergency*?

- (F) in a newspaper
- (G) in a history book
- (H) in a dictionary
- (J) in an encyclopedia

5. Where would you look to find information about today's weather?

- (A) in a newspaper
- (B) in a history book
- (C) in a dictionary
- (D) in an encyclopedia

6. Where would you look to find out who was the twelfth President?

- (F) in a newspaper
- (G) in a magazine
- (H) in a dictionary
- (J) in an encyclopedia

GO ON

LANGUAGE: STUDY SKILLS

● **Lesson 13: Study Skills (cont.)**

Directions: Read the Table of Contents and Index. Then answer the questions.

TABLE OF CONTENTS		INDEX	
Chapter 1: Animals Around the World 11		anteaters	12, 14–15
Chapter 2: Zoos of the World 42		black widow spiders	114, 118
Chapter 3: Creatures of the Sea 59		crocodiles	103–107
Chapter 4: Rodents 85		mice	89–93
Chapter 5: Reptiles and Amphibians 101		deer mice	90
Chapter 6: Insects and Spiders 112		house mice	92–93
		rainforest animals	39–41
		whales	60–64
		blue whales	62
		killer whales	64

 **Clue** Remember, a table of contents gives you the names of chapters or topics, and an index shows you where specific information is found.

● **Practice**

7. **In which chapter would you look for information about butterflies?**
    - (A) Chapter 3
    - (B) Chapter 4
    - (C) Chapter 5
    - (D) Chapter 6

8. **There is some information about mice on page—**
    - (F) 15
    - (G) 105
    - (H) 90
    - (J) 55

9. **To find out about rainforest animals, turn to pages—**
    - (A) 60–64
    - (B) 103–107
    - (C) 39–41
    - (D) 14–15

10. **Which chapter would you read to learn about rats?**
    - (F) Chapter 1
    - (G) Chapter 2
    - (H) Chapter 3
    - (J) Chapter 4

11. **If you wanted information on blue whales, you would turn to page—**
    - (A) 60
    - (B) 61
    - (C) 62
    - (D) 64

12. **Where would you look to find information about the Seattle Zoo?**
    - (F) Chapter 1
    - (G) Chapter 2
    - (H) Chapter 3
    - (J) Chapter 4

 GO ON

LANGUAGE: STUDY SKILLS

● Lesson 13: Study Skills (cont.)

13. Which word comes first in the dictionary?

- Ⓐ bless
- Ⓑ belt
- Ⓒ bear
- Ⓓ blue

14. Which word comes first in the dictionary?

- Ⓕ ditch
- Ⓖ dine
- Ⓗ din
- Ⓙ dial

15. Which word comes first in the dictionary?

- Ⓐ creek
- Ⓑ cross
- Ⓒ crabby
- Ⓓ crease

16. Which word comes first in the dictionary?

- Ⓕ market
- Ⓖ mark
- Ⓗ make
- Ⓙ mar

17. Look at the guide words. Which word would be found on the page?

- Ⓐ clock
- Ⓑ climate
- Ⓒ clear
- Ⓓ clog

guide words
clean–cliff

18. Look at the guide words. Which word would be found on the page?

- Ⓕ empire
- Ⓖ enchant
- Ⓗ engrave
- Ⓙ enter

guide words
empty–enemy

Use the dictionary entries and the pronunciation guide to answer questions 19–20.

save [sāv] v. 1. to rescue from harm or danger. 2. to keep in a safe condition. 3. to set aside for future use; store.

saving [sā′ vǐng] n. 1. rescuing from harm or danger. 2. avoiding excess spending; economy. 3. something saved.

savory [sā′ və-rē] adj. 1. appealing to the taste or smell. 2. salty to the taste; not sweet.

Pronunciation Guide
act, wāy, dâre, ärt, set, ēqual, big, ĭce, box, ōver, hôrse, bŏŏk, tōōl, us, tûrn

Note: (upside-down *e*) = *a* in alone, *e* in mitten, *o* in actor, *u* in circus

19. The *a* in the word *saving* sounds most like the word—

- Ⓐ pat
- Ⓑ ape
- Ⓒ heated
- Ⓓ naughty

20. Which sentence uses *savory* as in definition number 2?

- Ⓕ After I ate the savory stew, I was thirsty.
- Ⓖ The savory bank opened an account for me.
- Ⓗ This flower has a savory scent.
- Ⓙ The savory dog rescued me from harm.

STOP

Name _____ Date_____

Directions: Read each item. Choose the answer that you think is correct.

Examples

A. Which of these words comes first in the dictionary?

- (A) full
- (B) fulfill
- (C) fume
- (D) fuel

B. Where would you look to find the phone number for a store?

- (F) in a newspaper
- (G) in a telephone book
- (H) in a dictionary
- (J) in an atlas

---

1. Which of these words comes first in the dictionary?

- (A) lettuce
- (B) let
- (C) lean
- (D) leak

2. Which of these words comes first in the dictionary?

- (F) cheese
- (G) chess
- (H) cheat
- (J) chalk

3. Which of these words comes first in the dictionary?

- (A) slipper
- (B) slink
- (C) slip
- (D) slim

4. Where would you look to find out how yesterday is broken into syllables?

- (F) in a newspaper
- (G) in a history book
- (H) in a dictionary
- (J) in an encyclopedia

5. Where would you look to find a map of Oregon?

- (A) in a newspaper
- (B) in an atlas
- (C) in a telephone book
- (D) in a math book

6. Where would you look to find the address and telephone number of a restaurant?

- (F) in a newspaper
- (G) in a telephone book
- (H) in a dictionary
- (J) in an encyclopedia

7. Look at the guide words. Which word would be found on the page?

- (A) minute
- (B) minnow
- (C) misty
- (D) mysterious

guide words
mint–mist

8. Look at the guide words. Which word would be found on the page?

- (F) petticoat
- (G) pen
- (H) pair
- (J) pardon

guide words
part–pet

GO ON →

For numbers 9–12, look at the index page for the letter O. Then answer the questions.

O	
Oak,	291–292
Obsidian,	175–176
Oceans,	361–375
density in,	363–364
life in,	367–370
waves,	371–372
temperatures of,	365
resources,	373–375

9. **What information will you find on page 365?**
   - (A) ocean temperatures
   - (B) density of the ocean
   - (C) waves
   - (D) ocean life

10. **On what pages will you most likely find out about mining in the ocean for minerals?**
    - (F) pages 175–176
    - (G) pages 368–369
    - (H) pages 373–375
    - (J) pages 371–372

11. **You can read about octopuses on pages 368–369. In which section of Oceans is this?**
    - (A) resources
    - (B) life in
    - (C) waves
    - (D) temperatures

12. **On what pages would you find information about oak trees?**
    - (F) pages 175–176
    - (G) pages 291–292
    - (H) pages 361–375
    - (J) pages 376–399

Use the dictionary entry to answer questions 13–14.

beam [bēm] n. 1. a squared-off log used to support a building. 2. a ray of light. 3. the wooden roller in a loom. v. 1. to shine. 2. to smile broadly.

13. **Which use of the word *beam* is a verb?**
    - (A) The beam held up the plaster ceiling.
    - (B) The beam of light warmed the room.
    - (C) She moved the beam before she added a row of wool.
    - (D) The bright shells beam in the sand.

14. **Which sentence uses the word *beam* as in the first definition of the noun?**
    - (F) The ceiling beam had fallen into the room.
    - (G) The beam of the loom was broken.
    - (H) She beamed her approval.
    - (J) The beam of sunlight came through the tree.

STOP

═══ LANGUAGE: WRITING ═══

● Lesson 14: Writing

Directions: On a separate sheet of paper, write a response to each prompt. Include all the parts in the checklists.

1.   Write an Opinion

Write about your favorite book. Tell why you like it. Tell why someone else should like it, too.

Checklist:

Read what you wrote. Did you remember to do the following?

	Yes	No
Clearly state your opinion.	☐	☐
Give good reasons for your opinion. Organize your reasons.	☐	☐
Use words and phrases such as *because*, *therefore*, *since*, and *for example* to link your reasons with your opinion.	☐	☐
Write a strong ending.	☐	☐

2.   Write an Opinion

Write to ask your parent, teacher, principal, or someone else for something you really want. Give reasons why you want it.

Checklist:

Read what you wrote. Did you remember to do the following?

	Yes	No
Clearly state your opinion.	☐	☐
Give good reasons for your opinion. Organize your reasons.	☐	☐
Use words and phrases such as *because*, *therefore*, *since,* and *for example* to link your reasons with your opinion.	☐	☐
Write a strong ending.	☐	☐

3.   Write to Inform

Write step-by-step directions for something you know how to do well, such as hitting a ball or playing a card game.

Checklist:

Read what you wrote. Did you remember to do the following?

	Yes	No
Introduce your topic.	☐	☐
Use facts, definitions, examples, and details.	☐	☐
Organize information into categories.	☐	☐
Use words such as *also*, *another*, *and, more,* and *but* to link ideas.	☐	☐
Write a strong ending.	☐	☐

GO ON →

LANGUAGE: WRITING

● Lesson 14: Writing (cont.)

4. Write to Inform

Write about something you observed. Describe it in detail.

Checklist:

Read what you wrote. Did you remember to do the following?

	Yes	No
Introduce your topic.	☐	☐
Use facts, definitions, examples, and details.	☐	☐
Organize information into categories.	☐	☐
Use words such as *also*, *another*, *and, more*, and *but* to link ideas.	☐	☐
Write a strong ending.	☐	☐

5. Write a Narrative

Write a tall tale about why something is the way it is. For example, make up a story to explain why the sky is blue or why it rains in the spring.

Checklist:

Read what you wrote. Did you remember to do the following?

	Yes	No
Establish the situation, and introduce the narrator.	☐	☐
Describe the characters, setting, and plot of your story.	☐	☐

	Yes	No
Use dialogue and descriptions to show how characters think, feel, and act.	☐	☐
Use words such as *next* or *then* to explain events in the order they happen.	☐	☐
Write a strong ending.	☐	☐

6. Write a Narrative

Write to tell the story of someone's life. Tell when and where the person lived and what he or she did.

Checklist:

Read what you wrote. Did you remember to do the following?

	Yes	No
Establish the situation, and introduce the narrator.	☐	☐
Describe the characters, setting, and plot of your story.	☐	☐
Use dialogue and descriptions to show how characters think, feel, and act.	☐	☐
Use words such as *next* or *then* to explain events in the order they happen.	☐	☐
Write a strong ending.	☐	☐

LANGUAGE PRACTICE TEST
Part 1: Language Mechanics

Examples

For A and numbers 1–5, choose the answer that shows the correct punctuation mark. If no punctuation is missing, choose the answer "None."

A.   My uncle lives in Paris France.

- (A) .
- (B) ,
- (C) !
- (D) None

For B and numbers 6–8, choose the answer that shows the correct punctuation.

B.   The store _____ on Fort Street.

- (F) wasn't
- (G) wasnt
- (H) was'nt
- (J) wasn't'

---

1.   Is that your house

- (A) .
- (B) ,
- (C) ?
- (D) None

2.   Mr Sanchez is a lawyer.

- (F) .
- (G) ?
- (H) !
- (J) None

3.   Don't touch that

- (A) ,
- (B) ?
- (C) !
- (D) None

4.   The old dog slept in the sun.

- (F) .
- (G) ?
- (H) !
- (J) None

5.   We moved here from Seattle Washington.

- (A) ,
- (B) .
- (C) !
- (D) None

For numbers 6–8, choose the answer that shows the correct punctuation.

6.   _____ you Jason's cousin?

- (F) Aren't
- (G) Arent
- (H) Are'nt
- (J) Arent'

7.   _____ walk on the grass.

- (A) Dont
- (B) Don't
- (C) Dont'
- (D) Do'nt

8.   _____ better at math than I am.

- (F) Youre
- (G) Your'e
- (H) Youre'
- (J) You're

GO ON

LANGUAGE PRACTICE TEST
Part 1: Language Mechanics (cont.)

For numbers 9–13, choose the answer that shows a capital letter that is missing.

9.
- (A) he walked
- (B) to the store
- (C) to buy milk.
- (D) None

10.
- (F) My aunt
- (G) is named
- (H) aunt Tilly.
- (J) None

11.
- (A) On our trip
- (B) to France,
- (C) we saw Roman ruins.
- (D) None

12.
- (F) My mother
- (G) wrote a book,
- (H) *The ocean and You.*
- (J) None

13.
- (A) My brothers
- (B) are named
- (C) Jared and Jamal.
- (D) None

For numbers 14–17, choose the answer that shows the correct capitalization.

14. **Did you start school on _____?**
- (F) tuesday morning
- (G) Tuesday morning
- (H) Tuesday Morning
- (J) tuesday Morning

15. **Ms. Wu is my _____.**
- (A) favorite teacher
- (B) Favorite teacher
- (C) favorite Teacher
- (D) Favorite Teacher

16. **Isn't that zoo in _____?**
- (F) San francisco
- (G) San Francisco
- (H) san francisco
- (J) san Francisco

17. **Math is my _____.**
- (A) best Subject
- (B) Best Subject
- (C) Best subject
- (D) best subject

GO ON

Name _____   Date _____

For numbers 18–22, read the passage. Then answer the questions. The passage has underlined phrases, and the questions will ask about them. Choose "Correct as it is" if the underlined part of the sentence is correct.

(1) <u>Yellowstone park is</u> known for its geysers. (2) A geyser is formed when water is trapped under the <u>ground melted rock</u> heats the water. (3) When the water boils, it shoots through a hole and high into the air. (4) <u>There are more than 300 geysers in Yellowstone.</u> (5) The best-known geyser is called <u>old faithful.</u> (6) It is as faithful as a clock. (7) <u>Old Faithfuls fame</u> makes it the most visited geyser in Yellowstone Park.

18. In Sentence 1, <u>Yellowstone park is</u> best written—

   (F) yellowstone park
   (G) Yellowstone Park
   (H) YellowStone Park
   (J) Correct as it is

19. In Sentence 2, <u>ground melted rock is</u> best written—

   (A) ground. Melted rock
   (B) ground, melted rock
   (C) ground melted. Rock
   (D) Correct as it is

20. In Sentence 4, <u>There are more than 300 geysers in Yellowstone.</u> is best written—

   (F) There are More than 300 geysers in Yellowstone.
   (G) There are more than 300 geysers. In Yellowstone.
   (H) There are more than 300 geysers in yellowstone.
   (J) Correct as it is

21. In Sentence 5, <u>old faithful</u> is best written—

   (A) old Faithful
   (B) Old faithful
   (C) Old Faithful
   (D) Correct as it is

22. In Sentence 7, <u>Old Faithfuls fame</u> is best written—

   (F) Old Faithfuls' fame
   (G) old Faithful's fame
   (H) Old Faithful's fame
   (J) Correct as it is

LANGUAGE PRACTICE TEST

Part 2: Language Expression

Examples

Read each item. For A and numbers 1–4, choose the word that completes the sentence best.

A. The _____ plants are on the windowsill.

- (A) more pretty
- (B) prettier
- (C) prettiest
- (D) most prettier

For B and numbers 5–7, choose the answer that is a correct and complete sentence.

B.
- (F) Find we a map of this town.
- (G) I think us are lost!
- (H) We should have turned right on Mason Street.
- (J) Drive more slower so we can find the street.

---

1. Please lend _____ your mittens.

- (A) her
- (B) she
- (C) its
- (D) they

2. Don't _____ in the hallway.

- (F) running
- (G) ran
- (H) run
- (J) had run

3. The vine _____ up the side of the house.

- (A) climbing
- (B) climbs
- (C) did climbing
- (D) climb

4. Dr. and Mrs. Brown _____ the school last Monday.

- (F) visiting
- (G) visit
- (H) visits
- (J) visited

5.
- (A) Basketball was first thinked up by a teacher.
- (B) He needed a game for students to play indoors in the winter.
- (C) He nails a basket to the wall and made up a set of rules.
- (D) I think him had an idea that we all can enjoy!

6.
- (F) Bird watchers sometimes see birds taking dust baths.
- (G) The birds use the dust like them bathtub.
- (H) The dust helps they get rid of tiny bigs in their feathers.
- (J) The birds is smart to do this.

7.
- (A) The sunflower can be up to a foot wide.
- (B) It's petals are yellow.
- (C) They stem of this flower is very tall.
- (D) Some sunflowers is twice as tall as children.

GO ON

LANGUAGE PRACTICE TEST
Part 2: Language Expression (cont.)

For numbers 8–12, choose the answer that has the simple subject of the sentence underlined.

8.
- (F) The brave firefighters are always ready to go.
- (G) A loud bell rings.
- (H) The firefighters get into their red truck.
- (J) A spotted dog runs after the truck.

9.
- (A) I like to take care of my garden.
- (B) The black crows want to eat my corn.
- (C) The little rabbit wants to eat my carrots.
- (D) Even my silly dog likes to dig in my garden.

10.
- (F) My best friend Ed likes to play baseball.
- (G) My two cousins like to play, too.
- (H) We play on a team together.
- (J) The baseball games start next week.

11.
- (A) The Golden Gate Bridge was built across a large bay
- (B) Two towers hold up the bridge.
- (C) Giant cables hang between the towers.
- (D) This special bridge is famous.

12.
- (F) People built bridges long ago, just like they do today.
- (G) One kind of bridge that was used was a rope bridge.
- (H) The Romans built some stone bridges.
- (J) All kinds of bridges helped people in their daily lives.

For numbers 13–17, choose the answer choice that has the mistake. If all choices are correct, choose "No mistakes."

13.
- (A) The running shoes
- (B) wasn't the right size,
- (C) so I returned them.
- (D) No mistakes

14.
- (F) A baby kangaroo
- (G) lives in its mothers pouch
- (H) for nine months.
- (J) No mistakes

15.
- (A) Josh ran back
- (B) to mason Park
- (C) to look for his gloves.
- (D) No mistakes

16.
- (F) I was worried
- (G) that I did badly
- (H) on the history test.
- (J) No mistakes

17.
- (A) Jerry went over
- (B) to Jeff's house
- (C) to played computer games.
- (D) No mistakes

GO ON

LANGUAGE PRACTICE TEST
Part 2: Language Expression (cont.)

For numbers 18–20, choose the best combination of the underlined sentences.

18. **Mr. Lee is my teacher. Mr. Lee teaches third grade.**

    (F) Mr. Lee teachers third grade and he is my teacher.

    (G) Mr. Lee is my teacher and he teaches third grade.

    (H) Mr. Lee is my teacher for third grade.

    (J) Mr. Lee, teaches third grade, is my teacher.

19. **Chang went downtown. Chang went to the store.**

    (A) Chang went to the store and Chang went downtown.

    (B) Chang went to the store and downtown.

    (C) Chang, who went downtown, went to the store.

    (D) Chang went downtown to the store.

20. **You may play outside. You may play after you clean your room.**

    (F) After you clean your room, you may play outside.

    (G) You may play outside, but you may play after you clean your room.

    (H) You may play after you clean your room, outside.

    (J) Playing outside, you may after you clean your room.

For numbers 21–23, choose the best version of the sentence.

21. (A) On Saturday, we went to Grant Park for a picnic.

    (B) To Grant Park we went, on Saturday, for a picnic.

    (C) We went, for a picnic, to Grant Park on Saturday.

    (D) For a picnic, we went on Saturday to Grant Park.

22. (F) On the hill, Mr. Juarez lives in the house with the big garden.

    (G) Mr. Juarez lives in the house with the big garden, on the hill.

    (H) Mr. Juarez lives in the house on the hill with the big garden.

    (J) With the big garden, Mr. Juarez lives in the house on the hill.

23. (A) The firefly gives off light, but it does not give off heat.

    (B) The firefly gives off light but not heat.

    (C) The firefly, which does not give off heat, gives off light.

    (D) Gives off light, the firefly does not give off heat.

GO ON

Name _____ Date_____

Read the essay. Use the information to answer questions 24–27.

(1) Snowflakes look like white stars falling from the sky. (2) But there have been times when snow has looked red, green, yellow, and even black. (3) Black snow in France one year. (4) Another year, gray snow fell in Japan. (5) To make this dark snow, snow had mixed with ashes to make it. (6) Red snow that fell one year was made of snow mixed with red clay dust. (7) Most snow looks white. (8) It is really the color of ice. (9) Each snowflake begins with a small drop of frozen water. (10) When that water is mixed with some other material, the result is strangely colored snow.

24. Sentence 5 is best written—

  (F) Snow had mixed with ashes to make this dark snow.

  (G) Snow mixed with ashes was how this snow was made into dark snow.

  (H) To make this dark snow, it had ashes mixed with it.

  (J) Correct as it is

25. Which is not a complete sentence?

  (A) Sentence 1

  (B) Sentence 2

  (C) Sentence 3

  (D) Sentence 4

26. How could Sentences 7 and 8 best be joined together?

  (F) Really the color of ice, most snow looks white.

  (G) The color of ice, most snow is really white.

  (H) Most snow looks white and it is really the color of ice.

  (J) Most snow looks white, but it is really the color of ice.

27. Choose a topic sentence for this paragraph.

  (A) Think how it would seem to have colored snowflakes coming down around you.

  (B) Black snow in France scared the citizens.

  (C) Snow is always white, but it is really the color of ice.

  (D) Drops of frozen water make snow.

LANGUAGE PRACTICE TEST
Part 3: Spelling

Examples

For A and numbers 1–4, choose the word that fits into the sentence and is spelled correctly.

A.   He is _____ with us.

- (A) anoyed
- (B) annoyed
- (C) annoied
- (D) anoied

For B and numbers 5–8, choose the word that is spelled incorrectly. If all of the words are spelled correctly, choose "No mistakes."

B.
- (F) blankit
- (G) crater
- (H) footstep
- (J) No mistakes

---

1. **Please remember to _____ your homework.**
   - (A) compleet
   - (B) compleit
   - (C) complete
   - (D) compete

2. **The _____ is from the Ice Age.**
   - (F) glasier
   - (G) glacer
   - (H) glaceer
   - (J) glacier

3. **Henry was in the _____.**
   - (A) hospital
   - (B) hospitle
   - (C) hospittle
   - (D) hospitel

4. **Did you _____ the movie star?**
   - (F) recognise
   - (G) recognize
   - (H) recagnize
   - (J) recegnise

5.
- (A) sigh
- (B) merchent
- (C) moral
- (D) No mistakes

6.
- (F) league
- (G) hockey
- (H) meer
- (J) No mistakes

7.
- (A) churn
- (B) cottage
- (C) cadet
- (D) No mistakes

8.
- (F) cristal
- (G) faraway
- (H) afford
- (J) No mistakes

GO ON

LANGUAGE PRACTICE TEST
Part 3: Spelling (cont.)

For numbers 9–16, choose the word that is spelled incorrectly. If all of the words are spelled correctly, choose "No mistakes."

9.
- (A) curl
- (B) nerse
- (C) further
- (D) No mistakes

10.
- (F) writer
- (G) cofee
- (H) score
- (J) No mistakes

11.
- (A) wrist
- (B) resess
- (C) lazy
- (D) No mistakes

12.
- (F) finger
- (G) addition
- (H) supar
- (J) No mistakes

13.
- (A) dangerous
- (B) passenger
- (C) nature
- (D) No mistakes

14.
- (F) flask
- (G) puzzle
- (H) vegatable
- (J) No mistakes

15.
- (A) pickel
- (B) knick
- (C) witch
- (D) No mistakes

16.
- (F) reaf
- (G) geese
- (H) queen
- (J) No mistakes

For numbers 17–22, read each sentence. Look for the underlined word that is spelled incorrectly and choose that phrase. Choose "No mistakes" if the sentence is all correct.

17.
- (A) The fir on a rabbit's feet
- (B) gives the rabbit
- (C) the ability to hop on the snow.
- (D) No mistakes

18.
- (F) Some farmers
- (G) raize worms
- (H) as a crop.
- (J) No mistakes

19.
- (A) You can bake apples,
- (B) make applesauce,
- (C) or create delicious pies.
- (D) No mistakes

20.
- (F) Traffick signs
- (G) that are colored yellow
- (H) warn of changes ahead.
- (J) No mistakes

21.
- (A) Ancient drawings
- (B) show the Romans and Greeks
- (C) buying candy at shops.
- (D) No mistakes

22.
- (F) The stilt bird
- (G) has thin, red legs
- (H) and black feithers.
- (J) No mistakes

STOP

LANGUAGE PRACTICE TEST

● **Part 4: Study Skills**

Directions: For numbers A, B, and 1–8, choose the answer you think is correct.

Examples

A. **Which of these words comes first in the dictionary?**

(A) damp
(B) darn
(C) dale
(D) den

B. **Look at the guide words. Which word would be found on the page?**

(F) arctic
(G) ape
(H) aster
(J) assure

guide words
apple–assume

---

1. **Which of these words comes first in the dictionary?**

(A) tiger
(B) tin
(C) tiny
(D) tine

2. **Which of these words comes first in the dictionary?**

(F) this
(G) thirty
(H) thirsty
(J) thirteen

3. **Which of these words comes first in the dictionary?**

(A) city
(B) cider
(C) cinder
(D) cliff

4. **Which of these words comes first in the dictionary?**

(F) interesting
(G) indeed
(H) insurance
(J) idea

5. **Which of these words comes first in the dictionary?**

(A) trip
(B) trap
(C) tip
(D) truck

6. **Look at the guide words. Which word would be found on the page?**

(F) brute
(G) broken
(H) burn
(J) brake

guide words
branch–brown

7. **Look at the guide words. Which word would be found on the page?**

(A) puppy
(B) pet
(C) protect
(D) punish

guide words
prize–pump

8. **Look at the guide words. Which word would be found on the page?**

(F) stress
(G) strong
(H) straw
(J) strum

guide words
strawberry–stroll

GO ON

LANGUAGE PRACTICE TEST
Part 4: Study Skills (cont.)

For numbers 9–12, choose the answer that you think is correct.

9. **Where would you look to find the date of Memorial Day this year?**
   - (A) in a newspaper
   - (B) in a catalog
   - (C) in a dictionary
   - (D) on a calendar

10. **Where would you look to find a biography of Martin Luther King, Jr.?**
   - (F) in a newspaper
   - (G) in an atlas
   - (H) in an encyclopedia
   - (J) in a math book

11. **Where would you look to find the address of a school?**
   - (A) in a newspaper
   - (B) in a telephone book
   - (C) in a dictionary
   - (D) in an encyclopedia

12. **Which of these books would help you find out about becoming a pilot?**
   - (F) *The History of Flight*
   - (G) *Finding the Cheapest Airfares*
   - (H) *Learning to Fly and Navigate*
   - (J) *The Flight to the North Pole*

For numbers 13–16, read the Table of Contents. Then answer the questions.

TABLE OF CONTENTS
Chapter 1: Choosing Your Breed of Dog 11
Chapter 2: Selecting the Right Puppy 42
Chapter 3: Care and Feeding of Puppies 58
Chapter 4: Training Young Dogs 86
Chapter 5: Medical Care for Dogs 102
Chapter 6: Do You Have a Champion? 116

13. **A good title for this book might be—**
   - (A) *The Dog Owner's Manual*
   - (B) *Finding A Puppy of Your Own*
   - (C) *Champion Dog Breeds*
   - (D) *The History of Pets*

14. **To learn how to teach your dog to sit, turn to—**
   - (F) Chapter 1
   - (G) Chapter 2
   - (H) Chapter 3
   - (J) Chapter 4

15. **If you can't decide what kind of dog you want, turn to—**
   - (A) Chapter 1
   - (B) Chapter 2
   - (C) Chapter 3
   - (D) Chapter 4

16. **If your puppy seems to have a cold, turn to page—**
   - (F) 42
   - (G) 58
   - (H) 86
   - (J) 102

MATH: CONCEPTS

● Lesson 1: Numeration

Directions: Read and work each problem. Find the correct answer. Mark the space
for your choice.

Examples

A. Which of these is greater than 11?

- (A) 9
- (B) 5
- (C) 13
- (D) 10

B. What is another name for 72?

- (F) 7 tens and 3 ones
- (G) 8 tens and 0 ones
- (H) 7 tens and 7 ones
- (J) 7 tens and 2 ones

Clue Look for key words and numbers that will help you find
the answers.

● Practice

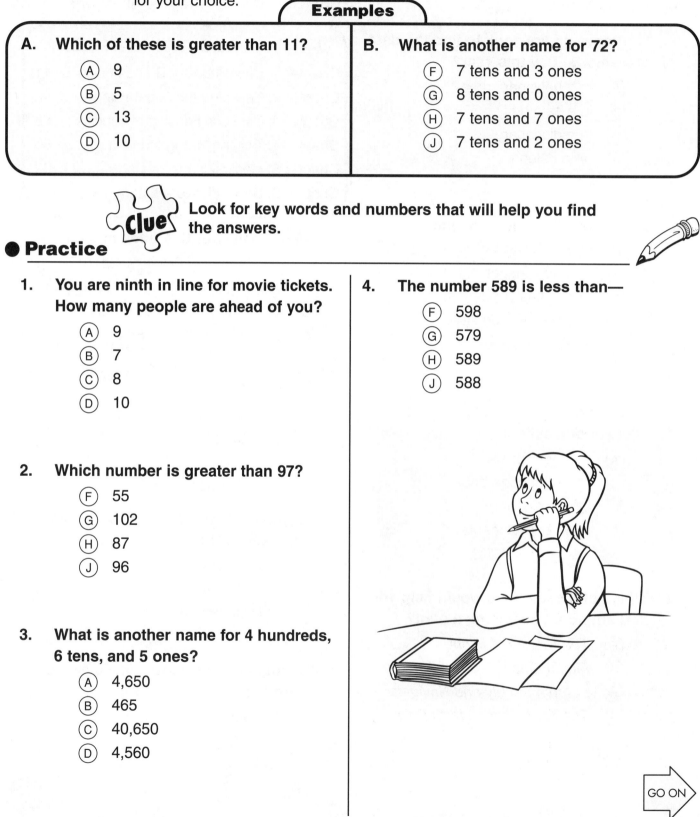

1. You are ninth in line for movie tickets.
   How many people are ahead of you?

   - (A) 9
   - (B) 7
   - (C) 8
   - (D) 10

2. Which number is greater than 97?

   - (F) 55
   - (G) 102
   - (H) 87
   - (J) 96

3. What is another name for 4 hundreds,
   6 tens, and 5 ones?

   - (A) 4,650
   - (B) 465
   - (C) 40,650
   - (D) 4,560

4. The number 589 is less than—

   - (F) 598
   - (G) 579
   - (H) 589
   - (J) 588

GO ON

MATH: CONCEPTS

● Lesson 1: Numeration (cont.)

Read and work each problem. Find the correct answer. Mark the space for your choice.

5. Which of these shows the same number of cats and dogs?

Ⓐ

Ⓑ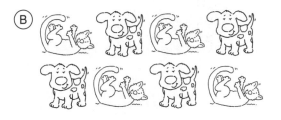

Ⓒ

Ⓓ

6. What is another name for 982?

　Ⓕ 9 thousands, 8 tens, and 2 ones

　Ⓖ 9 hundreds, 2 tens, and 8 ones

　Ⓗ 9 tens and 8 ones

　Ⓙ 9 hundreds, 8 tens, and 2 ones

7. How many of these numbers are greater than 218?

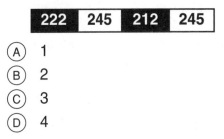

| 222 | 245 | 212 | 245 |

　Ⓐ 1

　Ⓑ 2

　Ⓒ 3

　Ⓓ 4

8. If you arranged these numbers from least to greatest, which number would be last?

| 1,012 | 1,022 | 1,002 | 1,021 |

　Ⓕ 1,012

　Ⓖ 1,021

　Ⓗ 1,022

　Ⓙ 1,002

9. How many hundreds are in 5,743?

　Ⓐ 5

　Ⓑ 3

　Ⓒ 4

　Ⓓ 7

10. The number 1,691 is less than—

　Ⓕ 1,609

　Ⓖ 1,699

　Ⓗ 1,690

　Ⓙ 1,600

11. How many thousands are in 9,482?

　Ⓐ 8

　Ⓑ 2

　Ⓒ 4

　Ⓓ 9

GO ON

━━━ MATH: CONCEPTS ━━━

● **Lesson 1: Numeration (cont.)**

Read and work each problem. Find the correct answer. Mark the space for your choice.

12. **What number goes into the box on the number line?**

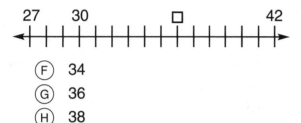

- Ⓕ 34
- Ⓖ 36
- Ⓗ 38
- Ⓙ 40

13. **What is another name for 651?**

- Ⓐ 6 thousands, 5 tens, and 1 ones
- Ⓑ 6 hundreds, 1 tens, and 5 ones
- Ⓒ 6 tens and 5 ones
- Ⓓ 6 hundreds, 5 tens, and 1 one

14. **Which of these numbers would come before 157 on a number line?**

- Ⓕ 159
- Ⓖ 147
- Ⓗ 165
- Ⓙ 158

15. **How many of these numbers are greater than 1,114?**

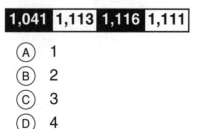

- Ⓐ 1
- Ⓑ 2
- Ⓒ 3
- Ⓓ 4

16. **How many hundreds are in 2,931?**

- Ⓕ 2
- Ⓖ 3
- Ⓗ 1
- Ⓙ 9

17. **How many thousands are in 6,517?**

- Ⓐ 5
- Ⓑ 1
- Ⓒ 6
- Ⓓ 7

18. **If a day's snowfall was between 1.01 inches and 2.32 inches, which of the measurements below might be the actual snowfall amount?**

- Ⓕ 1.00 inches
- Ⓖ 2.23 inches
- Ⓗ 2.52 inches
- Ⓙ 2.60 inches

MATH: CONCEPTS

● Lesson 2: Number Concepts

Directions: Read and work each problem. Find the correct answer. Mark the space for your choice.

Examples

A. Which of these is seventy-nine?

- Ⓐ 79
- Ⓑ 97
- Ⓒ 970
- Ⓓ 790

B. Which of these is an odd number?

- Ⓕ 424
- Ⓖ 12
- Ⓗ 317
- Ⓙ 76

Clue Look at any pictures or graphs carefully. When you are not sure of an answer, make your best guess and move on to the next problem.

● Practice

1. What number is represented by the chart?

Hundreds	Tens	Ones
I I I	I I I I I	I I I

- Ⓐ 335
- Ⓑ 533
- Ⓒ 353
- Ⓓ 335

2. What number is missing from the sequence?

6	12	18	____	30

- Ⓕ 20
- Ⓖ 24
- Ⓗ 22
- Ⓙ 26

3. Which of these is nine hundred sixty-four?

- Ⓐ 9,604
- Ⓑ 946
- Ⓒ 9,640
- Ⓓ 964

4. Find the answer that shows 35 peanuts.

GO ON

MATH: CONCEPTS

● Lesson 2: Number Concepts (cont.)

Read and work each problem. Find the correct answer. Mark the space for your choice.

5.

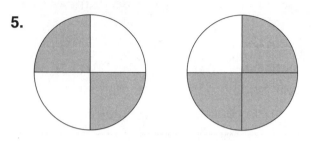

From the figures above, you know that—

Ⓐ $\frac{1}{3}$ is greater than $\frac{2}{3}$.

Ⓑ $\frac{1}{2}$ is greater than $\frac{3}{4}$.

Ⓒ $\frac{1}{2}$ is greater than $\frac{1}{4}$.

Ⓓ $\frac{3}{4}$ is greater than $\frac{1}{2}$.

6. 5 hundreds and 7 thousands equals—

Ⓕ 5,700

Ⓖ 7,050

Ⓗ 570

Ⓙ 7,500

7. Count by tens. Which number comes after 70 and before 90?

Ⓐ 50

Ⓑ 60

Ⓒ 80

Ⓓ 100

8. Which number below has a 9 in the hundreds place?

Ⓕ 5,967

Ⓖ 5,798

Ⓗ 9,654

Ⓙ 5,697

9. Which of these fractions is the largest?

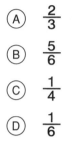

Ⓐ $\frac{2}{3}$

Ⓑ $\frac{5}{6}$

Ⓒ $\frac{1}{4}$

Ⓓ $\frac{1}{6}$

10. Which number is an odd number and can be divided by 5?

Ⓕ 30

Ⓖ 35

Ⓗ 40

Ⓙ 50

11. Which group of numbers has three odd numbers?

Ⓐ 8, 12, 15, 17, 20, 26, 30

Ⓑ 7, 10, 12, 13, 19, 22, 36

Ⓒ 2, 5, 8, 14, 18, 28, 32, 40

Ⓓ 16, 27, 28, 29, 30, 34, 38

12. How much of the circle below is shaded?

Ⓕ $\frac{5}{6}$

Ⓖ $\frac{2}{3}$

Ⓗ $\frac{1}{2}$

Ⓙ $\frac{1}{6}$

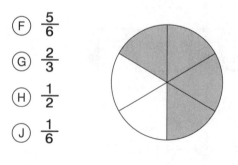

STOP

Name _____ Date _____

MATH: CONCEPTS

● Lesson 3: Properties

Directions: Read and work each problem. Find the correct answer. Mark the space
for your choice.

Examples

A. $12 + \square = 17$ $10 - \square = 5$
Which number completes both
number sentences above?

     Ⓐ 3
     Ⓑ 6
     Ⓒ 5
     Ⓓ 7

B. Which of these is 479 rounded to the
nearest hundred?

     Ⓕ 400
     Ⓖ 470
     Ⓗ 500
     Ⓙ 580

Clue Read each question carefully. If you are working on scrap
paper, be sure to read your notes carefully, too.

● Practice

1. $26 - \square = 17$ $31 + \square = 40$
Which number completes both
number sentences above?

     Ⓐ 6
     Ⓑ 8
     Ⓒ 9
     Ⓓ 7

2. $22 + \square = 29$ $16 - \square = 9$
Which number completes both
number sentences above?

     Ⓕ 5
     Ⓖ 9
     Ⓗ 7
     Ⓙ 6

3. Which of these is closest in
value to 190?

     Ⓐ 186
     Ⓑ 192
     Ⓒ 179
     Ⓓ 199

4. Which of these is 288 rounded to the
nearest hundred?

     Ⓕ 200
     Ⓖ 300
     Ⓗ 280
     Ⓙ 380

GO ON

Published by Spectrum. Copyright protected.   978-1-62057-595-6 *Spectrum Test Practice 3*

━━━━━ MATH: CONCEPTS ━━━━━

● **Lesson 3: Properties (cont.)**

Read and work each problem. Find
the correct answer. Mark the space
for your choice.

5. Which number sentence shows how
to find the total number of feathers?

    Ⓐ 3 + 4

    Ⓑ 3 ÷ 4

    Ⓒ 4 − 3

    Ⓓ 4 x 3

6. Round these numbers to the nearest
hundred: 575, 612, 499, 633, 590, 680.
How many of them will be 600?

    Ⓕ 3

    Ⓖ 4

    Ⓗ 5

    Ⓙ 6

7. 18 □ 9 = 9

Which operation sign belongs in the
box above?

    Ⓐ +

    Ⓑ −

    Ⓒ x

    Ⓓ ÷

8. 27 □ 8 = 19   10 □ 2 = 8

Which operation sign belongs in both
boxes above?

    Ⓕ +

    Ⓖ −

    Ⓗ x

    Ⓙ ÷

9. 0.8 =

    Ⓐ $\frac{1}{8}$

    Ⓑ $\frac{8}{100}$

    Ⓒ $\frac{80}{100}$

    Ⓓ $\frac{8}{10}$

10. Which number sentence would
you use to estimate 97 x 9 to the
nearest 100?

    Ⓕ 90 x 5

    Ⓖ 100 x 10

    Ⓗ 90 x 10

    Ⓙ 100 x 5

11. $\frac{1}{2} = \frac{3}{\square}$

What does the □ equal?

    Ⓐ 2

    Ⓑ 5

    Ⓒ 4

    Ⓓ 6

MATH: CONCEPTS

● **Lesson 4: Properties of Operations**

Directions: Choose the best answer for each question.

Examples

A. Drew bought 6 packs of trading cards. Each pack had 7 cards. He gave away 9 cards. How many cards did Drew have left?

- (A) 33
- (B) 42
- (C) 22
- (D) 51

B. What is the rule for the table?

IN	OUT
1	9
2	18
3	27
4	36

- (F) OUT = 8 + IN
- (G) OUT = 16 + IN
- (H) OUT = 9 × IN
- (J) OUT = 8 × IN

● **Practice**

1. Jaclyn sold 4 bags of 6 bagels. She also sold 5 individual bagels. Which equation could be used to find out how many bagels she sold in all?

- (A) (4 x 6) + 5
- (B) (4 x 5) + 6
- (C) 5(4 + 6)
- (D) 4(5 − 4)

2. The rule for this table is OUT = 6 + IN.

IN	OUT
5	11
7	13
9	15
11	17

If the IN number is an odd number, the OUT number will always be

- (F) a multiple of 2.
- (G) even.
- (H) a multiple of 5.
- (J) odd.

3. What is the rule for the table?

IN	OUT
35	5
42	6
49	7
56	8

- (A) OUT = 7 + IN
- (B) OUT = IN ÷ 7
- (C) OUT = 1 + IN
- (D) OUT = IN − 30

4. Marla had $3. She sold 7 marbles to her friends for 5 cents each. Then, she bought some gum for 79 cents. How much money does Marla have now?

- (F) $4.14
- (G) $3.35
- (H) $2.21
- (J) $2.56

MATH: CONCEPTS

● Lesson 5: Multiplication and Division

Directions: Choose the best answer for each question.

Examples

A. Carla has 4 shelves with books. Each shelf has 7 books. How many books are on Carla's shelves?

- (A) 14 books
- (B) 24 books
- (C) 28 books
- (D) 32 books

B. Miguel folds 16 T-shirts. He puts the T-shirts into 2 equal piles. How many T-shirts are in each pile?

- (F) 8 T-shirts
- (G) 4 T-shirts
- (H) 2 T-shirts
- (J) 14 T-shirts

● Practice

1. Which is equal to 5×7?

- (A) the number of miles driven in a week if one drives 5 miles each day
- (B) the amount of money left when spending $5 of $7
- (C) the weight of sand in each pile when dividing 7 pounds into 5 equal piles
- (D) the number of pencils when there are 5 more than 7 pencils

2. Which equation has a missing number that is equal to $72 \div 9$?

- (F) $9 \times 72 = \square$
- (G) $9 \times \square = 72$
- (H) $\square \div 72 = 9$
- (J) $\square \div 9 = 72$

3. Which number makes the equation $56 \div \square = 8$ true?

- (A) 6
- (B) 7
- (C) 8
- (D) 9

4. Mr. Patel wants to share 45 cookies equally with 9 people. Which equation can be used to determine how many cookies each person gets?

- (F) $45 \times \square = 9$
- (G) $9 \times 45 = \square$
- (H) $\square \div 45 = 9$
- (J) $45 \div 9 = \square$

5. $1 \times 6 \times 0 = \square$

- (A) 1
- (B) 6
- (C) 7
- (D) 0

GO ON

978-1-62057-595-6 *Spectrum Test Practice 3*

MATH: CONCEPTS

● Lesson 5: Multiplication and Division (cont.)

6. Ms. Henry secures a package using 3 pieces of tape. Each piece is 9 inches long. How many inches of tape does Ms. Henry use for one package?

  (F) 12 inches
  (G) 18 inches
  (H) 24 inches
  (J) 27 inches

7. Which multiplication expression will help find the answer to 18 ÷ 3?

  (A) 3 × 6
  (B) 3 × 8
  (C) 3 × 9
  (D) 3 × 18

8. $6 \times (4 + 9) = \square$

  (F) 78
  (G) 54
  (H) 72
  (J) 24

9. Find the missing number in the equation.
  $2 \times \square = 10$

  (A) 8
  (B) 6
  (C) 5
  (D) 4

10. Elizabeth has 3 bags of dried fruit. In total, the bags have 30 pieces of fruit. How many pieces of fruit are in each bag?

  (F) 30
  (G) 27
  (H) 15
  (J) 10

11. Which equation has a missing number that is equal to 12 ÷ 2?

  (A) $12 \div \square = 2$
  (B) $\square \div 12 = 2$
  (C) $12 \times \square = 2$
  (D) $2 \times 12 = \square$

12. $16 \div (8 - 0) = \square$

  (F) 0
  (G) 1
  (H) 2
  (J) 4

13. Find the missing number in the equation.
  $36 \div \square = 6$

  (A) 8
  (B) 6
  (C) 5
  (D) 4

14. A restaurant owner buys 4 boxes of glasses. Each box has 10 glasses. How many glasses does the owner buy?

  (F) 14 glasses
  (G) 10 glasses
  (H) 20 glasses
  (J) 40 glasses

GO ON

MATH: CONCEPTS

● Lesson 5: Multiplication and Division (cont.)

15. A store sells 32 boxes of tissues. Each person who buys tissues buys 4 boxes. How many people buy tissues at the store?

- Ⓐ 8
- Ⓑ 7
- Ⓒ 6
- Ⓓ 4

16. At a garage, a worker can change the oil in 5 cars in one hour. If there are 4 workers changing oil, how many cars can have their oil changed in one hour?

- Ⓕ 16 cars
- Ⓖ 15 cars
- Ⓗ 20 cars
- Ⓙ 25 cars

17. There are 5 buses taking students on a school trip. Each bus has 3 adults riding with the students. Which equation can be used to determine how many adults ride in the buses on the school trip?

- Ⓐ 3(5 − 3)
- Ⓑ 5(3 + 3)
- Ⓒ 5 + 3
- Ⓓ 5 x 3

18. Which multiplication expression will help find the answer to 48 ÷ 8?

- Ⓕ 8 × 4
- Ⓖ 8 × 5
- Ⓗ 8 × 6
- Ⓙ 8 × 7

19. Find the missing number in the equation.

□ ÷ 8 = 10

- Ⓐ 18
- Ⓑ 2
- Ⓒ 40
- Ⓓ 80

20. 49 ÷ (7 − 6) = □

- Ⓕ 49
- Ⓖ 7
- Ⓗ 42
- Ⓙ 1

21. Jordan has 14 baseballs that she wants to share evenly with her brother. Which equation could be used to find out how many baseballs each will have?

- Ⓐ 14 ÷ 2
- Ⓑ 14 − 2
- Ⓒ 14 + 2
- Ⓓ 14 × 2

22. Russ buys 5 packages of pencils. Each package has 8 pencils. Which expression shows how to find how many pencils Russ buys?

- Ⓕ 5 + 8
- Ⓖ 5 × 8
- Ⓗ 5 + 5 + 5 + 5 + 5
- Ⓙ 8 + 8 + 8 + 8

STOP

MATH: CONCEPTS

● **Lesson 6: Understanding Fractions**

Directions: Choose the best answer for each question.

Examples

A. **Which part is shaded?**

(A) $\frac{3}{1}$

(B) $\frac{1}{3}$

(C) $\frac{3}{4}$

(D) $\frac{1}{4}$

B. **What fraction is shown by point A?**

(F) $\frac{1}{8}$

(G) $\frac{1}{7}$

(H) $\frac{3}{8}$

(J) $\frac{3}{7}$

● **Practice**

1. **What fraction is shown by point F?**

(A) $\frac{1}{8}$

(B) $\frac{1}{7}$

(C) $\frac{1}{6}$

(D) $\frac{1}{5}$

2. **Which part is shaded?**

(F) $\frac{3}{8}$

(G) $\frac{3}{10}$

(H) $\frac{3}{12}$

(J) $\frac{3}{15}$

3. **What fraction is shown by point P?**

(A) $\frac{1}{3}$

(B) $\frac{2}{3}$

(C) $\frac{1}{2}$

(D) $\frac{2}{2}$

4. **Which part is shaded?**

(F) $\frac{2}{4}$

(G) $\frac{2}{6}$

(H) $\frac{4}{6}$

(J) $\frac{4}{2}$

5. **What fraction is shown by point B?**

(A) $\frac{1}{9}$

(B) $\frac{1}{10}$

(C) $\frac{1}{11}$

(D) $\frac{1}{12}$

6. **Which part is shaded?**

(F) $\frac{1}{6}$

(G) $\frac{5}{6}$

(H) $\frac{4}{6}$

(J) $\frac{6}{6}$

GO ON

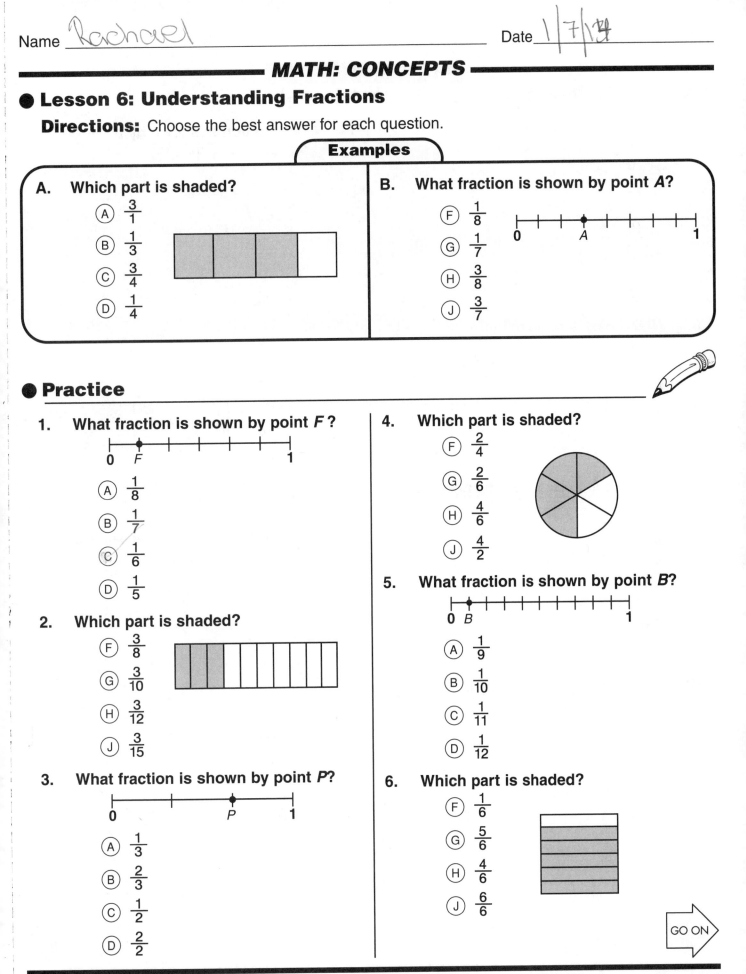

MATH: CONCEPTS

● **Lesson 6: Understanding Fractions (cont.)**

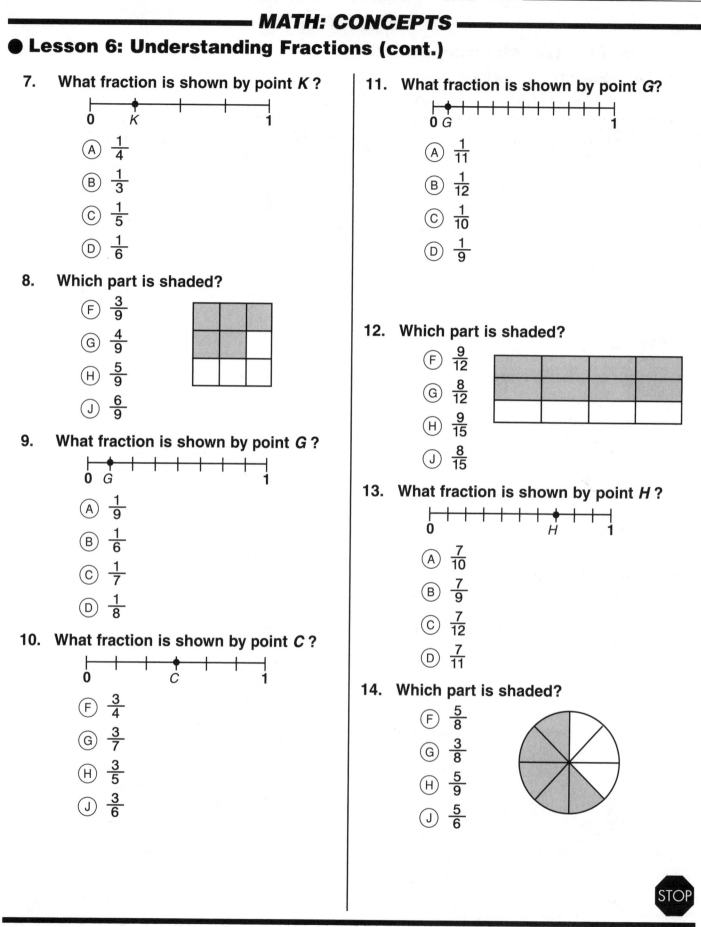

7. **What fraction is shown by point K?**

   (A) $\frac{1}{4}$

   (B) $\frac{1}{3}$

   (C) $\frac{1}{5}$

   (D) $\frac{1}{6}$

8. **Which part is shaded?**

   (F) $\frac{3}{9}$

   (G) $\frac{4}{9}$

   (H) $\frac{5}{9}$

   (J) $\frac{6}{9}$

9. **What fraction is shown by point G?**

   (A) $\frac{1}{9}$

   (B) $\frac{1}{6}$

   (C) $\frac{1}{7}$

   (D) $\frac{1}{8}$

10. **What fraction is shown by point C?**

    (F) $\frac{3}{4}$

    (G) $\frac{3}{7}$

    (H) $\frac{3}{5}$

    (J) $\frac{3}{6}$

11. **What fraction is shown by point G?**

    (A) $\frac{1}{11}$

    (B) $\frac{1}{12}$

    (C) $\frac{1}{10}$

    (D) $\frac{1}{9}$

12. **Which part is shaded?**

    (F) $\frac{9}{12}$

    (G) $\frac{8}{12}$

    (H) $\frac{9}{15}$

    (J) $\frac{8}{15}$

13. **What fraction is shown by point H?**

    (A) $\frac{7}{10}$

    (B) $\frac{7}{9}$

    (C) $\frac{7}{12}$

    (D) $\frac{7}{11}$

14. **Which part is shaded?**

    (F) $\frac{5}{8}$

    (G) $\frac{3}{8}$

    (H) $\frac{5}{9}$

    (J) $\frac{5}{6}$

STOP

MATH: CONCEPTS

● Lesson 7: Comparing Fractions

Directions: Choose the best answer for each question.

Examples

A. Which fraction is equivalent to $\frac{2}{3}$?

- (A) $\frac{6}{8}$
- (B) $\frac{5}{6}$
- (C) $\frac{3}{4}$
- (D) $\frac{4}{6}$

B. Which comparison is true?

- (F) $\frac{2}{3} > \frac{2}{4}$
- (G) $\frac{1}{2} > \frac{3}{2}$
- (H) $\frac{2}{3} < \frac{1}{3}$
- (J) $\frac{3}{6} < \frac{3}{8}$

● Practice

1. Which fraction is equivalent to 6?
   - (A) $\frac{1}{6}$
   - (B) $\frac{6}{6}$
   - (C) $\frac{6}{1}$
   - (D) $\frac{16}{1}$

2. Which fraction is equivalent to $\frac{1}{4}$?
   - (F) $\frac{2}{8}$
   - (G) $\frac{3}{8}$
   - (H) $\frac{2}{6}$
   - (J) $\frac{1}{2}$

3. Which is equivalent to $\frac{1}{2}$?

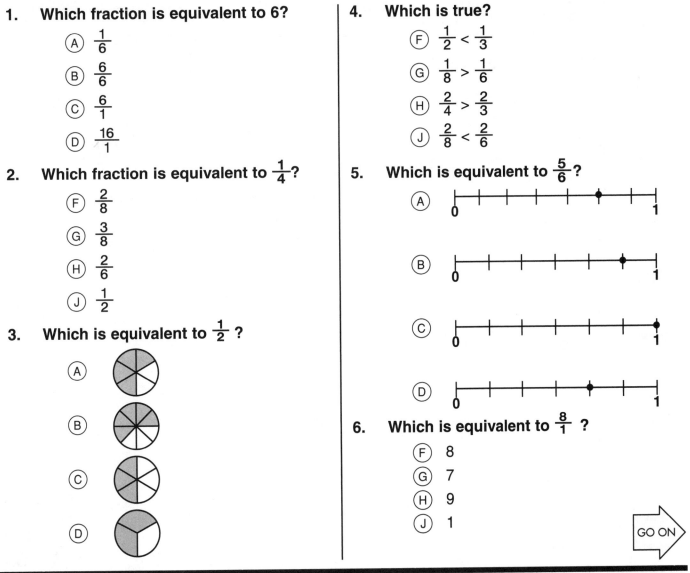

4. Which is true?
   - (F) $\frac{1}{2} < \frac{1}{3}$
   - (G) $\frac{1}{8} > \frac{1}{6}$
   - (H) $\frac{2}{4} > \frac{2}{3}$
   - (J) $\frac{2}{8} < \frac{2}{6}$

5. Which is equivalent to $\frac{5}{6}$?

6. Which is equivalent to $\frac{8}{1}$?
   - (F) 8
   - (G) 7
   - (H) 9
   - (J) 1

GO ON

     978-1-62057-595-6 *Spectrum Test Practice 3*

MATH: CONCEPTS

● Lesson 7: Comparing Fractions (cont.)

7. Which fraction is equivalent to $\frac{1}{3}$?
   - (A) $\frac{2}{3}$
   - (B) $\frac{2}{4}$
   - (C) $\frac{2}{6}$
   - (D) $\frac{2}{8}$

8. Which comparison is true?
   - (F) $\frac{3}{4} < \frac{2}{4}$
   - (G) $\frac{2}{6} < \frac{5}{6}$
   - (H) $\frac{3}{6} = \frac{5}{8}$
   - (J) $\frac{2}{4} = \frac{4}{6}$

9. Which fraction is equivalent to $\frac{1}{2}$?
   - (A) $\frac{2}{3}$
   - (B) $\frac{3}{4}$
   - (C) $\frac{3}{8}$
   - (D) $\frac{3}{6}$

10. Which fraction is equivalent to 10?
   - (F) $\frac{10}{1}$
   - (G) $\frac{1}{10}$
   - (H) $\frac{5}{5}$
   - (J) $\frac{10}{10}$

11. Which is equivalent to $\frac{2}{3}$?
   - (A)
   - (B)
   - (C)
   - (D)

12. Which comparison is true?
   - (F) $\frac{3}{6} > \frac{3}{8}$
   - (G) $\frac{1}{8} > \frac{1}{4}$
   - (H) $\frac{2}{3} < \frac{2}{6}$
   - (J) $\frac{3}{4} < \frac{1}{2}$

13. Which fraction is equivalent to $\frac{3}{4}$?
   - (A) $\frac{1}{2}$
   - (B) $\frac{2}{3}$
   - (C) $\frac{5}{6}$
   - (D) $\frac{6}{8}$

14. Which is equivalent to $\frac{7}{7}$?
   - (F) 1
   - (G) 2
   - (H) 7
   - (J) 14

STOP

978-1-62057-595-6 *Spectrum Test Practice 3*

Name _____   Date _____

MATH: CONCEPTS
SAMPLE TEST

Directions: Read and work each problem. Find the correct answer. Mark the space for your choice.

A. A squirrel had 15 acorns. He lost 7 of them. How can you find the number of acorns left?

- (A) add
- (B) subtract
- (C) multiply
- (D) divide

B. What is another name for 459?

- (F) 4 hundreds, 9 tens, and 5 ones
- (G) 4 hundreds, 5 tens, and 0 ones
- (H) 5 hundreds, 4 tens, and 9 ones
- (J) 4 hundreds, 5 tens, and 9 ones

---

1. You are number 12 in a line of 20 people. How many people are behind you?

- (A) 9
- (B) 7
- (C) 8
- (D) 6

2. What is another name for 8 hundreds, 4 tens, and 3 ones?

- (F) 8,430
- (G) 843
- (H) 834
- (J) 8,043

3. Which number is greater than 754?

- (A) 759
- (B) 749
- (C) 745
- (D) 744

4. The picture below shows the number of cars parked in a lot. Which answer is the same number as is shown in the picture?

- (F) 100 + 40 + 5
- (G) 1 + 4 + 5
- (H) 400 + 100 + 5
- (J) 4 + 10 + 5

5. The number 644 is less than—

- (A) 643
- (B) 654
- (C) 640
- (D) 634

6. How many tens are in 2,674?

- (F) 2
- (G) 6
- (H) 4
- (J) 7

GO ON

Name _____   Date_____

Read and work each problem. Find the correct answer. Mark the space for your choice.

7. What number is represented by the chart?

Hundreds	Tens	Ones
ⅠⅠⅠⅠⅠⅠ	ⅠⅠⅠⅠ ⅠⅠⅠⅠⅠ	ⅠⅠⅠⅠ

- Ⓐ 964
- Ⓑ 469
- Ⓒ 696
- Ⓓ 694

8. What number is missing from the sequence?

| 3 | 6 | ___ | 12 | 15 |

- Ⓕ 8
- Ⓖ 9
- Ⓗ 10
- Ⓙ 11

9. Paul and Vesta used a computer to solve a problem. Which of these is the same as the number on the screen?

- Ⓐ three thousand one hundred eighty
- Ⓑ three hundred eighty
- Ⓒ three thousand one hundred eight
- Ⓓ three thousand eighteen

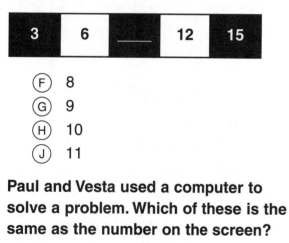

10. Round 3,322 to the nearest thousand.

- Ⓕ 4,000
- Ⓖ 3,300
- Ⓗ 3,000
- Ⓙ 4,300

11.

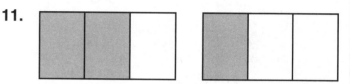

From the figures above, you know that—

- Ⓐ $\frac{1}{3}$ is greater than $\frac{2}{3}$.
- Ⓑ $\frac{1}{2}$ is greater than $\frac{2}{3}$.
- Ⓒ $\frac{2}{3}$ is greater than $\frac{1}{2}$.
- Ⓓ $\frac{2}{3}$ is greater than $\frac{1}{3}$.

12. Count by fives. Which number comes after 25 and before 35?

- Ⓕ 50
- Ⓖ 20
- Ⓗ 30
- Ⓙ 40

13. Which of these fractions is the largest?

- Ⓐ $\frac{2}{3}$
- Ⓑ $\frac{1}{2}$
- Ⓒ $\frac{1}{4}$
- Ⓓ $\frac{2}{5}$

GO ON

Published by Spectrum. Copyright protected.   116   978-1-62057-595-6 *Spectrum Test Practice 3*

MATH: CONCEPTS
SAMPLE TEST (cont.)

Read and work each problem. Find the correct answer. Mark the space for your choice.

14. Which number is an even number and can be divided evenly by 7?

    (F) 26
    (G) 35
    (H) 14
    (J) 60

15. Which number sentence shows how to find the total number of butterflies?

    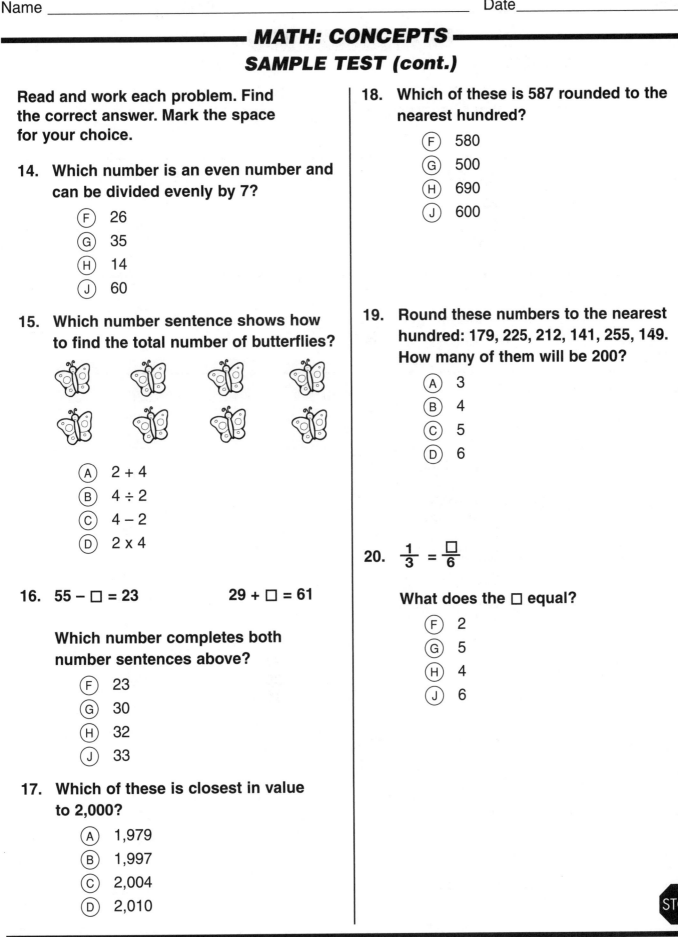

    (A) 2 + 4
    (B) 4 ÷ 2
    (C) 4 − 2
    (D) 2 x 4

16. 55 − ☐ = 23   29 + ☐ = 61

    Which number completes both number sentences above?

    (F) 23
    (G) 30
    (H) 32
    (J) 33

17. Which of these is closest in value to 2,000?

    (A) 1,979
    (B) 1,997
    (C) 2,004
    (D) 2,010

18. Which of these is 587 rounded to the nearest hundred?

    (F) 580
    (G) 500
    (H) 690
    (J) 600

19. Round these numbers to the nearest hundred: 179, 225, 212, 141, 255, 149. How many of them will be 200?

    (A) 3
    (B) 4
    (C) 5
    (D) 6

20. $\frac{1}{3} = \frac{\square}{6}$

    What does the ☐ equal?

    (F) 2
    (G) 5
    (H) 4
    (J) 6

STOP

MATH: COMPUTATION

● Lesson 8: Addition

Directions: Mark the space for the correct answer to each addition problem. Choose "None of these" if the right answer is not given.

Examples

A.
$$\begin{array}{r} 23 \\ + \ 4 \\ \hline \end{array}$$

- (A) 26
- (B) 25
- (C) 27
- (D) None of these

B. 39 + 21 =

- (F) 59
- (G) 61
- (H) 65
- (J) None of these

Clue The answer in an addition problem is always larger than the numbers being added.

● Practice

1.
$$\begin{array}{r} 37 \\ + 11 \\ \hline \end{array}$$

- (A) 44
- (B) 46
- (C) 48
- (D) None of these

2.
$$\begin{array}{r} 299 \\ + \ 54 \\ \hline \end{array}$$

- (F) 335
- (G) 353
- (H) 355
- (J) None of these

3. 12 + 29 + 6 =

- (A) 45
- (B) 49
- (C) 47
- (D) None of these

4. 33 + 33 + 33 =

- (F) 90
- (G) 96
- (H) 98
- (J) None of these

5.
$$\begin{array}{r} 519 \\ + \ 56 \\ \hline \end{array}$$

- (A) 575
- (B) 557
- (C) 577
- (D) None of these

6.
$$\begin{array}{r} 6.97 \\ + 1.62 \\ \hline \end{array}$$

- (F) 8.95
- (G) 8.59
- (H) 8.49
- (J) None of these

7.
$$\begin{array}{r} 270 \\ 955 \\ + 116 \\ \hline \end{array}$$

- (A) 1,343
- (B) 1,431
- (C) 1,340
- (D) None of these

8. 12 + 17 + 25 =

- (F) 45
- (G) 55
- (H) 54
- (J) None of these

GO ON

MATH: COMPUTATION

● Lesson 8: Addition (cont.)

Mark the space for the correct answer to each addition problem. Choose "None of these" if the right answer is not given.

9. $\frac{1}{6} + \frac{4}{6} =$

- Ⓐ $\frac{5}{12}$
- Ⓑ $\frac{1}{12}$
- Ⓒ $\frac{5}{6}$
- Ⓓ None of these

10. $39 + 21 + 44 =$

- Ⓕ 102
- Ⓖ 105
- Ⓗ 109
- Ⓙ None of these

11. $\begin{array}{r} 370 \\ + 119 \\ \hline \end{array}$

- Ⓐ 449
- Ⓑ 489
- Ⓒ 499
- Ⓓ None of these

12. $\begin{array}{r} 7{,}562 \\ + \ \ 177 \\ \hline \end{array}$

- Ⓕ 7,779
- Ⓖ 7,379
- Ⓗ 7,739
- Ⓙ None of these

13. $\$1.55 + \$2.39 =$

- Ⓐ $3.99
- Ⓑ $3.49
- Ⓒ $3.93
- Ⓓ None of these

14. $56 + 65 =$

- Ⓕ 121
- Ⓖ 112
- Ⓗ 211
- Ⓙ None of these

15. $\begin{array}{r} 555 \\ + \ \ 11 \\ \hline \end{array}$

- Ⓐ 1,100
- Ⓑ 1,001
- Ⓒ 1,010
- Ⓓ None of these

16. $\begin{array}{r} 4.56 \\ + \ 4.67 \\ \hline \end{array}$

- Ⓕ 9.13
- Ⓖ 9.23
- Ⓗ 9.32
- Ⓙ None of these

17. $\$20.09 + \$1.18 =$

- Ⓐ $21.17
- Ⓑ $20.27
- Ⓒ $21.27
- Ⓓ None of these

18. $11 + 12 + 13 =$

- Ⓕ 32
- Ⓖ 34
- Ⓗ 35
- Ⓙ None of these

STOP

MATH: COMPUTATION

● Lesson 9: Subtraction

Directions: Mark the space for the correct answer to each subtraction problem. Choose "None of these" if the right answer is not given.

Examples

A.
$$\begin{array}{r} 23 \\ -\ 5 \end{array}$$

- Ⓐ 16
- Ⓑ 18
- Ⓒ 20
- Ⓓ None of these

B. 49 – 12 =

- Ⓕ 37
- Ⓖ 27
- Ⓗ 39
- Ⓙ None of these

Clue When you are not sure about an answer, check it by adding.

● Practice

1.
$$\begin{array}{r} 62 \\ -\ 17 \end{array}$$

- Ⓐ 44
- Ⓑ 46
- Ⓒ 45
- Ⓓ None of these

5.
$$\begin{array}{r} 4.17 \\ -\ 0.50 \end{array}$$

- Ⓐ 3.67
- Ⓑ 3.77
- Ⓒ 3.66
- Ⓓ None of these

2.
$$\begin{array}{r} 200 \\ -\ 80 \end{array}$$

- Ⓕ 30
- Ⓖ 10
- Ⓗ 20
- Ⓙ None of these

6.
$$\begin{array}{r} 7.17 \\ -\ 1.62 \end{array}$$

- Ⓕ 5.45
- Ⓖ 5.57
- Ⓗ 5.55
- Ⓙ None of these

3. 55 – 5 – 9 =

- Ⓐ 40
- Ⓑ 41
- Ⓒ 42
- Ⓓ None of these

7.
$$\begin{array}{r} 9,550 \\ -\ 7,010 \end{array}$$

- Ⓐ 2,450
- Ⓑ 2,540
- Ⓒ 2,550
- Ⓓ None of these

4. 444 – 44 – 4 =

- Ⓕ 440
- Ⓖ 436
- Ⓗ 410
- Ⓙ None of these

8. 22 – 17 =

- Ⓕ 3
- Ⓖ 4
- Ⓗ 5
- Ⓙ None of these

GO ON

MATH: COMPUTATION

● Lesson 9: Subtraction (cont.)

Mark the space for the correct answer to each subtraction problem. Choose "None of these" if the right answer is not given.

9. $\frac{7}{9} - \frac{4}{9} =$
- (A) $\frac{3}{9}$
- (B) $\frac{3}{18}$
- (C) $\frac{11}{9}$
- (D) None of these

10. $0.39 - 0.12 =$
- (F) $0.20
- (G) $0.26
- (H) $0.29
- (J) None of these

11. $\begin{array}{r} 373 \\ -\ 369 \end{array}$
- (A) 2
- (B) 3
- (C) 4
- (D) None of these

12. $\begin{array}{r} 8,661 \\ -\ 120 \end{array}$
- (F) 8,441
- (G) 8,451
- (H) 8,541
- (J) None of these

13. $6.52 - 2.36 =$
- (A) $4.14
- (B) $4.15
- (C) $4.16
- (D) None of these

14. $98 - 89 =$
- (F) 7
- (G) 9
- (H) 8
- (J) None of these

15. $\begin{array}{r} 500 \\ -\ 50 \end{array}$
- (A) 400
- (B) 550
- (C) 50
- (D) None of these

16. $\begin{array}{r} 4.56 \\ -\ 4.52 \end{array}$
- (F) 0.40
- (G) 0.04
- (H) 9.38
- (J) None of these

17. $10.01 - 0.92 =$
- (A) $9.90
- (B) $9.01
- (C) $9.09
- (D) None of these

18. $\frac{5}{6} - \frac{4}{6} =$
- (F) $\frac{9}{6}$
- (G) $\frac{1}{6}$
- (H) $\frac{1}{12}$
- (J) None of these

STOP

MATH: COMPUTATION

● Lesson 10: Multiplication and Division

Directions: Mark the space for the correct answer to each problem. Choose "None of these" if the right answer is not given.

Examples

A.
$$\begin{array}{r} 3 \\ \times\ 4 \\ \hline \end{array}$$

- (A) 7
- (B) 10
- (C) 12
- (D) None of these

B. $10 \div 2 =$

- (F) 2
- (G) 4
- (H) 5
- (J) None of these

Clue Pay close attention to the operation sign in each question.

● Practice

1. $4 \times 0 =$
- (A) 0
- (B) 4
- (C) 8
- (D) None of these

5. $17 \div 8 =$
- (A) 2 R2
- (B) 2 R3
- (C) 2 R4
- (D) None of these

2. $6\overline{)13}$
- (F) 2
- (G) 2 R1
- (H) 2 R2
- (J) None of these

6. $4\overline{)200}$
- (F) 80
- (G) 50
- (H) 40
- (J) None of these

3.
$$\begin{array}{r} 7 \\ \times\ 10 \\ \hline \end{array}$$
- (A) 77
- (B) 17
- (C) 70
- (D) None of these

7.
$$\begin{array}{r} 210 \\ \times\ 5 \\ \hline \end{array}$$
- (A) 1,050
- (B) 1,500
- (C) 1,005
- (D) None of these

4. $4\overline{)36}$
- (F) 7
- (G) 8
- (H) 9
- (J) None of these

8. $10 \times \square = 20$
- (F) 1
- (G) 0
- (H) 2
- (J) None of these

GO ON

MATH: COMPUTATION

● Lesson 10: Multiplication and Division (cont.)

Mark the space for the correct answer to each problem. Choose "None of these" if the right answer is not given.

9. 201
    x 3
    - (A) 600
    - (B) 601
    - (C) 603
    - (D) None of these

10. 9 ÷ 9 =
    - (F) 1
    - (G) 2
    - (H) 3
    - (J) None of these

11. 4 x 11 =
    - (A) 40
    - (B) 44
    - (C) 48
    - (D) None of these

12. 0)$\overline{12}$
    - (F) 12
    - (G) 12 R1
    - (H) 0
    - (J) None of these

13. 12
    x 11
    - (A) 120
    - (B) 132
    - (C) 144
    - (D) None of these

14. 6)$\overline{68}$
    - (F) 11 R2
    - (G) 11 R3
    - (H) 11 R4
    - (J) None of these

15. 32 ÷ 4 =
    - (A) 6
    - (B) 2
    - (C) 4
    - (D) None of these

16. 4)$\overline{200}$
    - (F) 10
    - (G) 10 R1
    - (H) 11
    - (J) None of these

17. 300
    x 5
    - (A) 1,000
    - (B) 1,500
    - (C) 5,000
    - (D) None of these

18. 12 x □ = 48
    - (F) 2
    - (G) 3
    - (H) 4
    - (J) None of these

STOP

MATH: COMPUTATION

● **Lesson 11: Rounding Whole Numbers**

Directions: Choose the best answer for each question.

Example

A. Which is 349 rounded to the nearest ten?

(A) 300
(B) 340
(C) 350
(D) 400

● **Practice**

1. Which would round to 710 if rounded to the nearest ten?
   (A) 708
   (B) 715
   (C) 703
   (D) 719

2. Which is 489 rounded to the nearest hundred?
   (F) 400
   (G) 480
   (H) 490
   (J) 500

3. Which is 724 rounded to the nearest ten?
   (A) 700
   (B) 720
   (C) 730
   (D) 800

4. Which would round to 600 if rounded to the nearest hundred?
   (F) 658
   (G) 548
   (H) 691
   (J) 577

5. Which is 827 rounded to the nearest ten?
   (A) 800
   (B) 820
   (C) 830
   (D) 900

6. Which would not round to 300 if rounded to the nearest hundred?
   (F) 278
   (G) 301
   (H) 329
   (J) 247

7. Which is 692 rounded to the nearest ten?
   (A) 700
   (B) 690
   (C) 680
   (D) 600

8. Which would round to 470 if rounded to the nearest ten?
   (F) 462
   (G) 476
   (H) 371
   (J) 474

STOP

Name _____ Date _____

SAMPLE TEST

Directions: Mark the space for the correct answer to each problem. Choose "None of these" if the right answer is not given.

Examples

A.
$$555$$
$$+\ \ 99$$

  (A) 655
  (B) 456
  (C) 654
  (D) None of these

B. 78 − 39 =

  (F) 117
  (G) 39
  (H) 59
  (J) None of these

1.
$$444$$
$$-\ \ 66$$

  (A) 550
  (B) 510
  (C) 378
  (D) None of these

2. $\frac{4}{5} - \frac{1}{5} =$

  (F) $\frac{3}{5}$
  (G) $\frac{2}{5}$
  (H) $\frac{5}{5}$
  (J) None of these

3. $\frac{3}{4} - \frac{1}{4} =$

  (A) $\frac{2}{4}$
  (B) $\frac{1}{4}$
  (C) $\frac{4}{4}$
  (D) None of these

4. 65 + 61 + 7 =

  (F) 122
  (G) 123
  (H) 133
  (J) None of these

5.
$$9,000$$
$$-\ \ 5,010$$

  (A) 3,900
  (B) 3,909
  (C) 3,990
  (D) None of these

6.
$$6.98$$
$$-\ \ 1.55$$

  (F) 5.45
  (G) 5.57
  (H) 5.55
  (J) None of these

7.
$$519$$
$$+\ \ 56$$

  (A) 543
  (B) 545
  (C) 533
  (D) None of these

8. 35 − 19 =

  (F) 15
  (G) 17
  (H) 19
  (J) None of these

9. 10 + 31 + 8 =

  (A) 50
  (B) 49
  (C) 47
  (D) None of these

GO ON

Name _____   Date_____

Mark the space for the correct answer to each problem. Choose "None of these" if the right answer is not given.

10. $0.37 + $6.19 =
- (F) $6.56
- (G) $6.57
- (H) $6.47
- (J) None of these

11. 300
     x 5
- (A) 1,000
- (B) 1,500
- (C) 5,000
- (D) None of these

12. 12 x □ = 48
- (F) 2
- (G) 3
- (H) 4
- (J) None of these

13. 222
     + 11
- (A) 232
- (B) 231
- (C) 233
- (D) None of these

14. 3,904
     + 154
- (F) 4,185
- (G) 4,158
- (H) 4,058
- (J) None of these

15. $\frac{3}{4} - \frac{1}{4} =$
- (A) $\frac{2}{4}$
- (B) $\frac{1}{4}$
- (C) $\frac{4}{4}$
- (D) None of these

16. $1\overline{)50}$
- (F) 50
- (G) 5
- (H) 0
- (J) None of these

17. 93
     x 6
- (A) 99
- (B) 548
- (C) 558
- (D) None of these

18. $7\overline{)77}$
- (F) 10 R1
- (G) 11
- (H) 11 R1
- (J) None of these

19. 4,009
     − 27
- (A) 4,036
- (B) 3,982
- (C) 3,992
- (D) None of these

20. 5.91
     − 2.39
- (F) 8.30
- (G) 3.52
- (H) 3.62
- (J) None of these

21. $1\frac{4}{5} - \frac{1}{5} =$
- (A) 2
- (B) $1\frac{1}{5}$
- (C) $1\frac{3}{5}$
- (D) None of these

22. $2.00 − $1.17 =
- (F) $0.38
- (G) $0.88
- (H) $3.17
- (J) None of these

GO ON

MATH: COMPUTATION
SAMPLE TEST (cont.)

Mark the space for the correct answer to each problem. Choose "None of these" if the right answer is not given.

23. 6,788
    + 999

- (A) 5,789
- (B) 7,777
- (C) 7,787
- (D) None of these

24.   578
    + 34

- (F) 612
- (G) 613
- (H) 544
- (J) None of these

25. $\frac{3}{8} - \frac{1}{8} =$

- (A) $\frac{4}{8}$
- (B) $\frac{5}{8}$
- (C) $\frac{2}{8}$
- (D) None of these

26. $7\overline{)3,577}$

- (F) 500
- (G) 510 R1
- (H) 511
- (J) None of these

27. $5.67
    + $1.23

- (A) $6.90
- (B) $4.54
- (C) $4.44
- (D) None of these

28.   6.02
    + 3.91

- (F) 2.11
- (G) 9.93
- (H) 9.91
- (J) None of these

29.   84
     x 11

- (A) 920
- (B) 924
- (C) 824
- (D) None of these

30. $10\overline{)100}$

- (F) 11
- (G) 10
- (H) 1
- (J) None of these

31. $\frac{1}{3} + \frac{2}{3} + 1 =$

- (A) $3\frac{1}{3}$
- (B) 2
- (C) 3
- (D) None of these

32. $12.00 − $3.91 =

- (F) $15.91
- (G) $8.01
- (H) $8.09
- (J) None of these

For numbers 33 and 34, choose the answer that goes in the box.

33. 11 x □ = 121

- (A) 10
- (B) 12
- (C) 11
- (D) None of these

34. 99 ÷ □ = 9

- (F) 9
- (G) 12
- (H) 10
- (J) None of these

STOP

Name _____ Date_____

==================== **MATH: APPLICATIONS** ====================

● **Lesson 12: Geometry**

Directions: Read and work each problem. Find the correct answer. Mark the space for your choice.

┌─────── **Example** ───────┐

A. Look at the picture of the castle made with blocks. Which shape was used only one time?

- (A) circle
- (B) triangle
- (C) rectangle
- (D) square

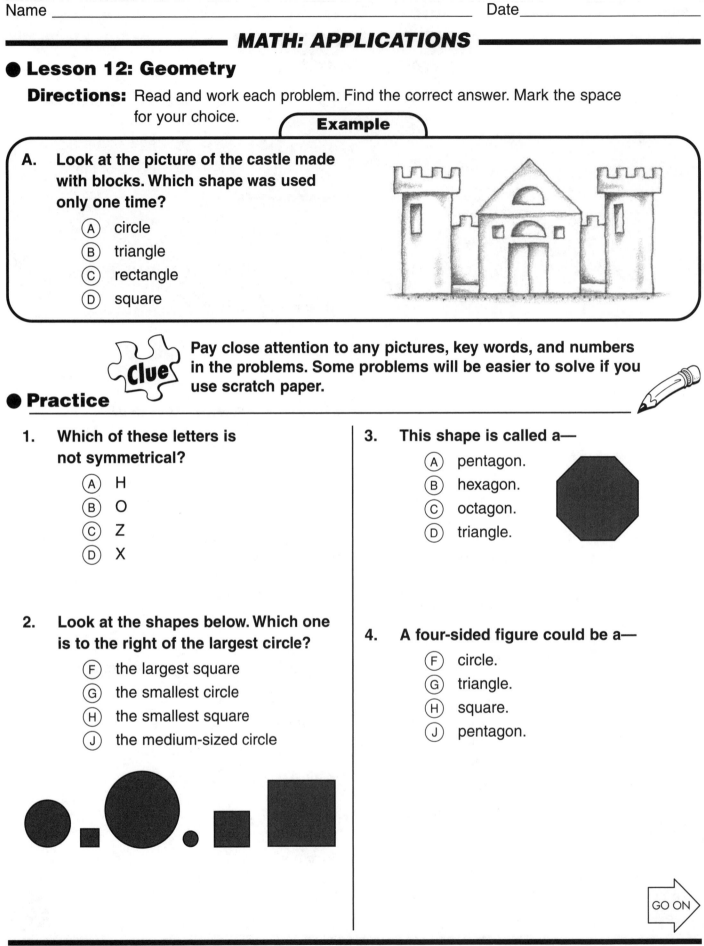

Clue Pay close attention to any pictures, key words, and numbers in the problems. Some problems will be easier to solve if you use scratch paper.

● **Practice**

1. Which of these letters is not symmetrical?
   - (A) H
   - (B) O
   - (C) Z
   - (D) X

2. Look at the shapes below. Which one is to the right of the largest circle?
   - (F) the largest square
   - (G) the smallest circle
   - (H) the smallest square
   - (J) the medium-sized circle

3. This shape is called a—
   - (A) pentagon.
   - (B) hexagon.
   - (C) octagon.
   - (D) triangle.

4. A four-sided figure could be a—
   - (F) circle.
   - (G) triangle.
   - (H) square.
   - (J) pentagon.

GO ON

MATH: APPLICATIONS

● **Lesson 12: Geometry (cont.)**

Read and work each problem. Find the correct answer. Mark the space for your choice.

5.   Which of these letters is symmetrical?

    Ⓐ   J
    Ⓑ   M
    Ⓒ   P
    Ⓓ   B

6.   Look at the picture of the tile floor. What is the area of the gray tiles?

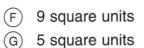

    Ⓕ   9 square units
    Ⓖ   5 square units
    Ⓗ   11 square units
    Ⓙ   10 square units

7.   This shape is called a—

    Ⓐ   circle.
    Ⓑ   sphere.
    Ⓒ   pentagon.
    Ⓓ   pyramid.

8.   Which of these figures is not the same shape and size as the others?

Ⓕ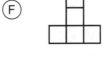

Ⓖ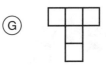

Ⓗ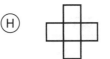

Ⓙ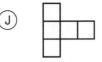

GO ON

● Lesson 12: Geometry (cont.)

Read and work each problem. Find the correct answer. Mark the space for your choice.

9. **What is the perimeter of the polygon?**

   Ⓐ   38 inches
   Ⓑ   26 inches
   Ⓒ   28 inches
   Ⓓ   Not enough information

   *7 inches   6 inches
   5 inches   9 inches
   11 inches*

10. **Look at the shaded area in this picture. If each square is an inch, what is the area of the shaded part?**

   Ⓕ   289 square inches
   Ⓖ   150 square inches
   Ⓗ   19 square inches
   Ⓙ   17 square inches

11. **If the perimeter of this figure is 88 inches, the missing side is—**

   *24 inches
   20 inches   20 inches*

   Ⓐ   12 inches long.
   Ⓑ   20 inches long.
   Ⓒ   24 inches long.
   Ⓓ   Not enough information

12. **Look at the figure. What is its area and perimeter?**

   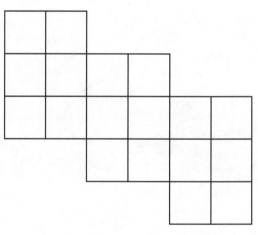

   Ⓕ   The area is 18 square units and the perimeter is 22 units.
   Ⓖ   The area is 22 square units and the perimeter is 14 units.
   Ⓗ   The area is 16 square units and the perimeter is 14 units.
   Ⓙ   Not enough information

   GO ON

MATH: APPLICATIONS

● **Lesson 12: Geometry (cont.)**

Read and work each problem. Find the correct answer. Mark the space for your choice.

13. **A basketball is shaped like a—**

   Ⓐ pyramid.
   Ⓑ circle.
   Ⓒ sphere.
   Ⓓ rectangle.

14. **A polygon that has 6 sides and 6 vertices is a—**

   Ⓕ pentagon.
   Ⓖ hexagon.
   Ⓗ octagon.
   Ⓙ trapezoid.

15. **The perimeter of this figure is—**

   Ⓐ 12 units.
   Ⓑ 20 units.
   Ⓒ 14 units.
   Ⓓ not enough information

16. **Which figure shows parallel lines?**

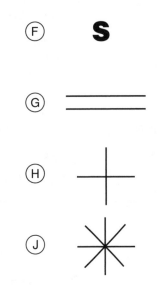

   Ⓕ **S**

   Ⓖ ═══

   Ⓗ ┼

   Ⓙ ✳

17. **A can of soup is shaped like a—**

   Ⓐ pyramid.
   Ⓑ sphere.
   Ⓒ cylinder.
   Ⓓ trapezoid.

18. **A polygon that only has one pair of parallel sides is a—**

   Ⓕ parallelogram.
   Ⓖ quadrilateral.
   Ⓗ hexagon.
   Ⓙ trapezoid.

STOP

MATH: APPLICATIONS

● Lesson 13: Shapes and Their Attributes

Directions: Use the words and pictures to solve each problem. Choose the best answer.

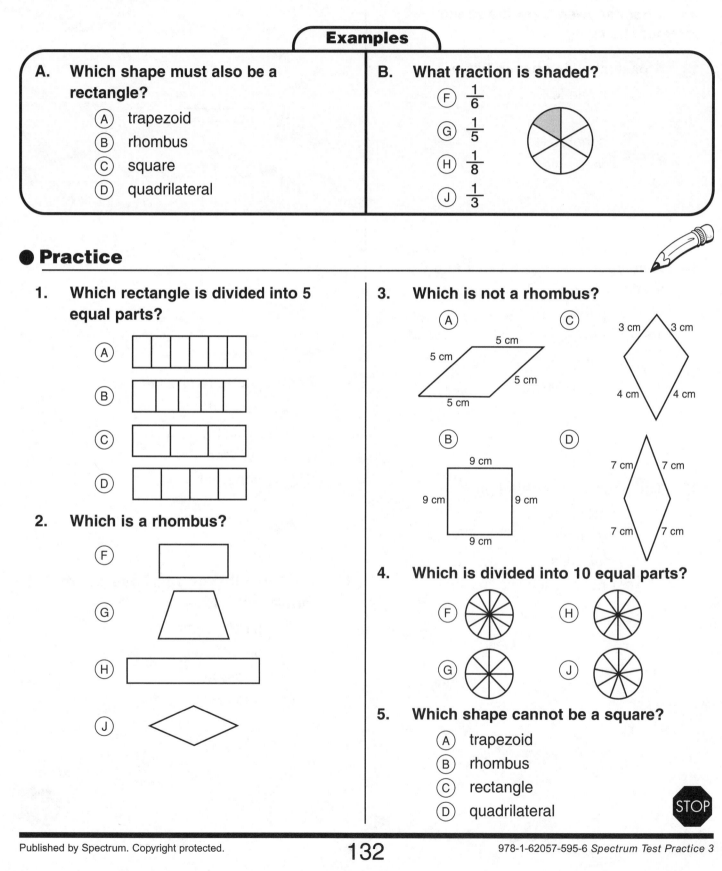

Examples

A. Which shape must also be a rectangle?

- Ⓐ trapezoid
- Ⓑ rhombus
- Ⓒ square
- Ⓓ quadrilateral

B. What fraction is shaded?

- Ⓕ $\frac{1}{6}$
- Ⓖ $\frac{1}{5}$
- Ⓗ $\frac{1}{8}$
- Ⓙ $\frac{1}{3}$

● Practice

1. Which rectangle is divided into 5 equal parts?

- Ⓐ
- Ⓑ
- Ⓒ
- Ⓓ

2. Which is a rhombus?

- Ⓕ
- Ⓖ
- Ⓗ
- Ⓙ

3. Which is not a rhombus?

- Ⓐ 5 cm / 5 cm / 5 cm / 5 cm
- Ⓒ 3 cm / 3 cm / 4 cm / 4 cm
- Ⓑ 9 cm / 9 cm / 9 cm / 9 cm
- Ⓓ 7 cm / 7 cm / 7 cm / 7 cm

4. Which is divided into 10 equal parts?

- Ⓕ
- Ⓗ
- Ⓖ
- Ⓙ

5. Which shape cannot be a square?

- Ⓐ trapezoid
- Ⓑ rhombus
- Ⓒ rectangle
- Ⓓ quadrilateral

STOP

MATH: APPLICATIONS

● Lesson 14: Measurement

Directions: Read and work each problem. Find the correct answer. Mark the space for your choice.

Example

A. **What time does the clock show?**

- (A) 9:45
- (B) 10:15
- (C) 10:45
- (D) 11:00

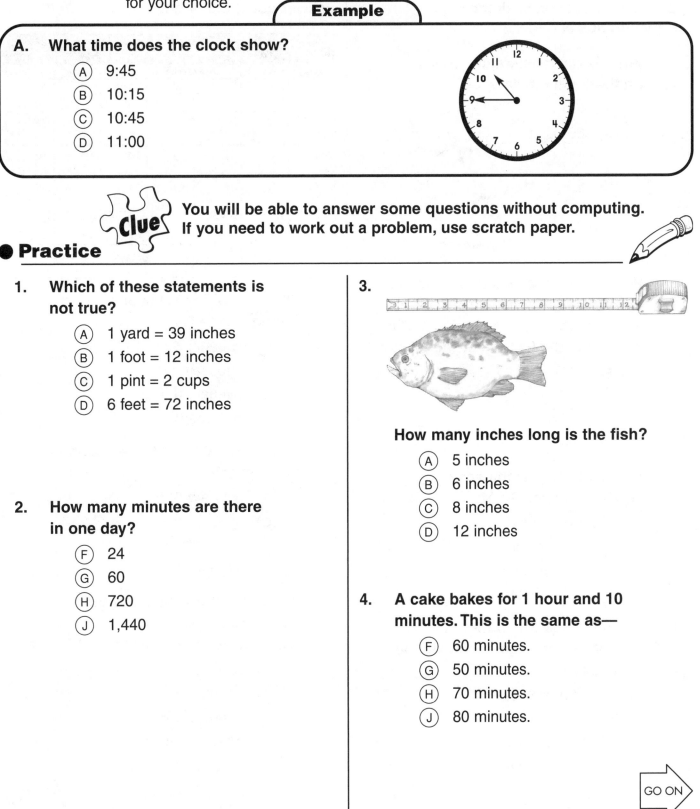

Clue You will be able to answer some questions without computing. If you need to work out a problem, use scratch paper.

● Practice

1. **Which of these statements is not true?**

- (A) 1 yard = 39 inches
- (B) 1 foot = 12 inches
- (C) 1 pint = 2 cups
- (D) 6 feet = 72 inches

2. **How many minutes are there in one day?**

- (F) 24
- (G) 60
- (H) 720
- (J) 1,440

3. **How many inches long is the fish?**

- (A) 5 inches
- (B) 6 inches
- (C) 8 inches
- (D) 12 inches

4. **A cake bakes for 1 hour and 10 minutes. This is the same as—**

- (F) 60 minutes.
- (G) 50 minutes.
- (H) 70 minutes.
- (J) 80 minutes.

GO ON

MATH: APPLICATIONS

● Lesson 14: Measurement (cont.)

Read and work each problem. Find the correct answer. Mark the space for your choice.

5. **What is the temperature shown on the thermometer?**

    Ⓐ 74° C
    Ⓑ 66° C
    Ⓒ 64° C
    Ⓓ 54° C

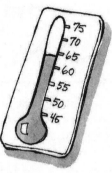

6. **Pedro painted a picture of a house during art class. He worked for 40 minutes. The art class ended at 2:00. What time did Pedro start his picture?**

    Ⓕ 1:30
    Ⓖ 1:20
    Ⓗ 1:10
    Ⓙ 1:40

7. **Which of these is the same as 10 millimeters?**

    Ⓐ 1 meter
    Ⓑ 1 kilometer
    Ⓒ 1 centimeter
    Ⓓ 1 decimeter

8. **It takes a plane 4 hours to fly from Detroit to Los Angeles. This is the same as—**

    Ⓕ 180 minutes.
    Ⓖ 200 minutes.
    Ⓗ 240 minutes.
    Ⓙ 360 minutes.

Use the calendar page for January to answer questions 9–11.

January						
Sunday	Monday	Tuesday	Wednesday	Thursday	Friday	Saturday
					1	2 Concert
3 Family party for Chung	4	5 Chung's birthday	6	7	8	9 Maria's sledding party
10	11 Teacher Conference	12	13	14	15	16
17 Go to Grandma's for dinner	18	19	20 Science Fair	21	22	23
24	25	26 Field trip	27	28 Winter break	29 Winter break	30
31						

9. **What day of the week is Chung's birthday?**

    Ⓐ January 5
    Ⓑ Tuesday
    Ⓒ January 3
    Ⓓ Saturday

10. **What is the date of the last Sunday of the month?**

    Ⓕ January 31
    Ⓖ January 24
    Ⓗ January 30
    Ⓙ January 17

11. **Chung's birthday is on January 5. If her book report was due on the following Tuesday, what date it is due?**

    Ⓐ January 19
    Ⓑ January 11
    Ⓒ January 18
    Ⓓ January 12

GO ON ⇨

MATH: APPLICATIONS

● Lesson 14: Measurement (cont.)

Read and work each problem. Find the correct answer. Mark the space for your choice.

12. What time does the clock show?

- F 7:30
- G 7:20
- H 7:25
- J 7:35

13. A student won a juggling contest, keeping all three balls in the air for 7 minutes. If she started at 1:35, what time did she finish juggling?

- A 1:44
- B 1:42
- C 1:43
- D 1:47

14. How much did the average daily temperature change from February to March?

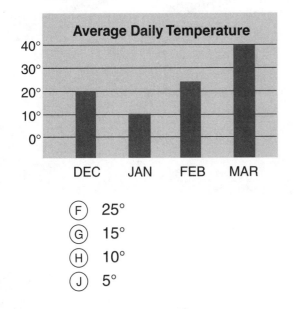

- F 25°
- G 15°
- H 10°
- J 5°

15. Tad wants to find the weight of a box of cereal. What unit of measurement will he probably find on the side of the box?

- A millimeters
- B pounds
- C hectoliters
- D ounces

16. If each of these nails were 1.5 centimeters long, how long would they be all together if you laid them end-to-end?

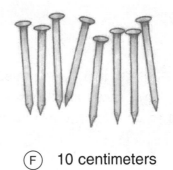

- F 10 centimeters
- G 11 centimeters
- H 12 centimeters
- J 13 centimeters

GO ON

MATH: APPLICATIONS

● **Lesson 14: Measurement (cont.)**

Read and work each problem. Find the correct answer. Mark the space for your choice.

17. **Carrie loves to go skating. She went outside with her friends at 3:00. At 4:20 they came back inside. For how long did they skate?**

    Ⓐ 60 minutes
    Ⓑ 50 minutes
    Ⓒ 70 minutes
    Ⓓ 80 minutes

18. **Which temperature would probably feel the most comfortable?**

    Ⓕ 20° F
    Ⓖ 35° F
    Ⓗ 90° F
    Ⓙ 70° F

19. **Look at the sign. If you just missed the 2:10 show, how many minutes will you need to wait for the next one?**

    AMAZING DOLPHIN SHOW!
    Daily at
    1:15
    2:10
    3:05
    4:00
    4:50

    Ⓐ 50 minutes
    Ⓑ 45 minutes
    Ⓒ 60 minutes
    Ⓓ 55 minutes

Use the calendar page to answer questions 20 and 21.

March						
Sunday	Monday	Tuesday	Wednesday	Thursday	Friday	Saturday
	1	2	3	4	5	6
7	8	9	10	11	12	13
14	15	16	17	18	19	20
21	22	23	24	25	26	27
28	29	30	31			

20. **What is the date of the last Wednesday of the month?**

    Ⓕ March 31
    Ⓖ March 30
    Ⓗ March 24
    Ⓙ March 29

21. **On what day does March 11 fall?**

    Ⓐ Wednesday
    Ⓑ Thursday
    Ⓒ Friday
    Ⓓ Saturday

MATH: APPLICATIONS

● Lesson 15: Finding Area

Directions: Choose the best answer for each question.

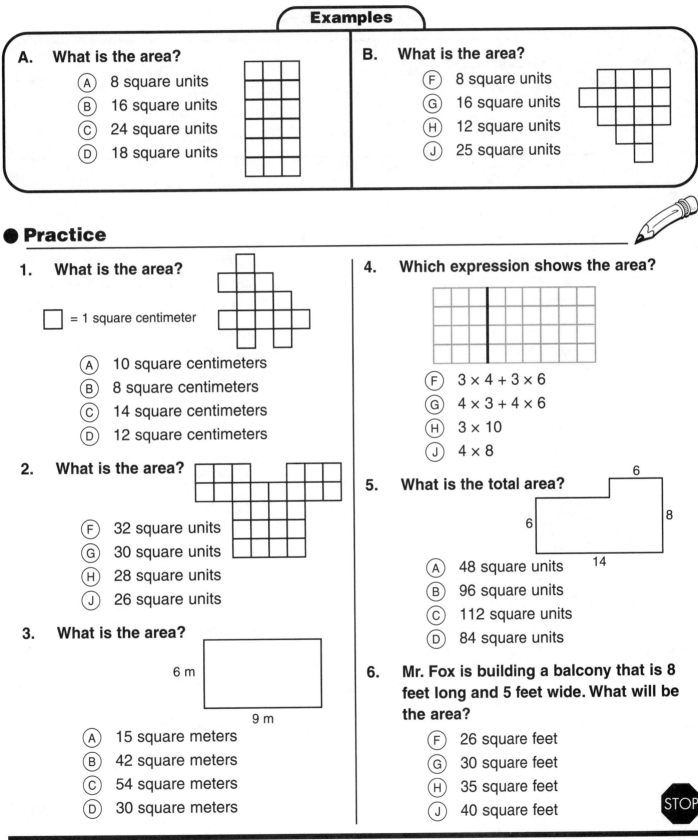

Examples

A.   What is the area?
- (A) 8 square units
- (B) 16 square units
- (C) 24 square units
- (D) 18 square units

B.   What is the area?
- (F) 8 square units
- (G) 16 square units
- (H) 12 square units
- (J) 25 square units

● Practice

1.   What is the area?

☐ = 1 square centimeter

- (A) 10 square centimeters
- (B) 8 square centimeters
- (C) 14 square centimeters
- (D) 12 square centimeters

2.   What is the area?
- (F) 32 square units
- (G) 30 square units
- (H) 28 square units
- (J) 26 square units

3.   What is the area?

6 m

9 m

- (A) 15 square meters
- (B) 42 square meters
- (C) 54 square meters
- (D) 30 square meters

4.   Which expression shows the area?
- (F) 3 × 4 + 3 × 6
- (G) 4 × 3 + 4 × 6
- (H) 3 × 10
- (J) 4 × 8

5.   What is the total area?

6

6   8

14

- (A) 48 square units
- (B) 96 square units
- (C) 112 square units
- (D) 84 square units

6.   Mr. Fox is building a balcony that is 8 feet long and 5 feet wide. What will be the area?
- (F) 26 square feet
- (G) 30 square feet
- (H) 35 square feet
- (J) 40 square feet

STOP

MATH: APPLICATIONS

● **Lesson 16: Mass and Liquid Volume**

Directions: Solve each problem. Choose the best answer.

Example

A. Which is the best estimate for the mass of a baby?	Ⓐ 4 kilograms
	Ⓑ 4 grams
	Ⓒ 40 kilograms
	Ⓓ 40 grams

● **Practice**

1. Harry buys a bag with 120 grams of trail mix. He gives 48 grams of trail mix to his sister. How much trail mix does Harry have left?

   Ⓐ 48 grams
   Ⓑ 82 grams
   Ⓒ 72 grams
   Ⓓ 24 grams

2. Which is the best estimate for the volume of a kitchen sink?

   Ⓕ 5 liters
   Ⓖ 50 liters
   Ⓗ 500 liters
   Ⓙ 5,000 liters

3. Darla buys 9 bottles of water. Each bottle holds 3 liters. How much water does Darla buy?

   Ⓐ 27 liters
   Ⓑ 24 liters
   Ⓒ 21 liters
   Ⓓ 18 liters

4. Darnell has a pile of nickels. The total mass of the nickels is 45 grams. If each nickel has a mass of 5 grams, how many nickels does Darnell have?

   Ⓕ 45 nickels
   Ⓖ 40 nickels
   Ⓗ 9 nickels
   Ⓙ 5 nickels

5. One bag of flour has a mass of 4 kilograms. What is the mass of 3 of these bags?

   Ⓐ 7 kilograms
   Ⓑ 8 kilograms
   Ⓒ 12 kilograms
   Ⓓ 15 kilograms

6. Which is the best estimate for the mass of a textbook?

   Ⓕ 4 grams
   Ⓖ 40 grams
   Ⓗ 400 grams
   Ⓙ 40 kilograms

MATH: APPLICATIONS

● Lesson 17: Problem Solving

Directions: Read and work each problem. Find the correct answer. Mark the space for your choice.

Example

A. There are 98 houses in Jan's neighborhood. She delivers the newspaper to all but 45 of them. How many papers does she deliver?

(A) 143
(B) 53
(C) 49
(D) 150

Clue Some questions will need more than one step to find an answer. Use scratch paper to help you keep track of the steps.

● Practice

Use the information below to help you solve numbers 1–3.

You have a bag of candy to share with your class. There are 25 students in your class. You want each student to get 7 pieces.

1. What operation will you need to use to figure out how many candies you need?

   (A) addition
   (B) subtraction
   (C) multiplication
   (D) division

2. How many candies do you have in all?

   (F) 200
   (G) 175
   (H) 1,500
   (J) 145

3. If two students are absent on the day you hand out the candies, how many will you have left over?

   (A) 10
   (B) 25
   (C) 12
   (D) 14

4. A tsunami is a wave created by underwater earthquakes. Tsunamis can reach heights of 37 meters. How many centimeters tall is that?

   (F) 37,000 centimeters
   (G) 3,700 centimeters
   (H) 370 centimeters
   (J) 3.70 centimeters

GO ON

MATH: APPLICATIONS

● **Lesson 17: Problem Solving (cont.)**

5. A worker at Command Software makes $720 a week. You want to figure out how much he makes an hour. What other piece of information do you need?

  (A) the number of weeks the worker works each year

  (B) the number of vacation days the worker takes

  (C) how much money the worker makes each day

  (D) how many hours a day the worker works

Read and work each problem. Find the correct answer. Mark the space for your choice.

Jimmy wants to buy baseball cards for his collection. At a sale, the cards are being sold in packs. Look at the chart below. Use it to answer questions 6–9.

Number of Packs	Number of Cards
2	16
4	32
6	___
7	56

6. What number sentence do you need to find the number of cards in each package?

  (F) 2 x 16

  (G) 16 − 2

  (H) 16 ÷ 2

  (J) 56 − 7

7. How many baseball cards are in each pack?

  (A) 5

  (B) 6

  (C) 7

  (D) 8

8. What is the missing number in the chart?

  (F) 38

  (G) 42

  (H) 48

  (J) Not enough information

9. If Jimmy bought 3 packs of baseball cards, how many cards would he have all together?

  (A) 18

  (B) 24

  (C) 32

  (D) 36

10. In the picture below, 1 book stands for 5 books. How many books does this picture stand for?

  (F) 25

  (G) 45

  (H) 40

  (J) 30

11. A single-scoop ice cream cone used to cost $1.39. The price has gone up 9 cents. How much does it cost now?

  (A) $1.42

  (B) $1.48

  (C) $1.58

  (D) $1.30

GO ON

MATH: APPLICATIONS

● Lesson 17: Problem Solving (cont.)

Read and work each problem. Find the correct answer. Mark the space for your choice.

12. What other equation belongs in the same fact family as 17 x 8 = 136?

- (F) 13 x 8 = 104
- (G) 136 ÷ 2 = 68
- (H) 8 x 17 = 136
- (J) 17 + 8 = 25

Read the information below. Use it to answer questions 13–15.

    Abraham and his friends Luke and Esther bought a large chocolate cake. Abraham cut it into 6 equal pieces. He shared the cake with his friends. Abraham had more than either Luke or Esther. Esther had more than Luke.

13. Who had the most cake?

- (A) Abraham
- (B) Luke
- (C) Esther
- (D) Not enough information

14. If Esther had 2 pieces, how many pieces did Abraham have?

- (F) 4
- (G) 3
- (H) 2
- (J) 1

15. If the cake cost $6.00 and the 3 friends split the cost equally, how much would they each pay?

- (A) $1.00
- (B) $2.00
- (C) $3.00
- (D) $4.00

16. A doctor has her office open 5 days a week, 8 hours a day. If she sees 4 patients an hour, how many patients does she see in 1 day?

- (F) 24
- (G) 28
- (H) 38
- (J) 32

17. In a desert garden, there are 6 rows of cactus plants. Each row has 5 plants. How many cactus plants are there in the garden?

- (A) 20
- (B) 25
- (C) 30
- (D) 35

GO ON

MATH: APPLICATIONS

● Lesson 17: Problem Solving (cont.)

Read and work each problem. Find the correct answer. Mark the space for your choice.

18. Jawan's sister has four coins. One is a nickel and one is a dime. Which of these amounts might she have?

   - (F) 15 cents
   - (G) 20 cents
   - (H) 24 cents
   - (J) 30 cents

19. A total of 60 people brought their pets to the show. Half the people bought dogs and 20 people brought cats. How many people brought other kinds of pets?

   - (A) 30
   - (B) 10
   - (C) 20
   - (D) 40

Look at the menu. Then answer questions 20–22.

MENU

Hamburger............$2.49

Cheeseburger........$2.89

Taco....................$1.35

Hot Dog...............$1.75

Cola....................$1.00

Lemonade............$1.10

20. Choose the lunch item that costs the most.

   - (F) hamburger
   - (G) cheeseburger
   - (H) taco
   - (J) hot dog

21. If you ordered a hamburger and lemonade, how much would they cost?

   - (A) $1.79
   - (B) $2.99
   - (C) $3.99
   - (D) $3.59

22. Choose the lunch that would cost the least.

   - (F) a taco and a lemonade
   - (G) a hamburger and a cola
   - (H) a hot dog and a cola
   - (J) a taco and a cola

STOP

MATH: APPLICATIONS

● **Lesson 18: Interpret Data**

Directions: Use the graphs to answer the questions.

● **Practice**

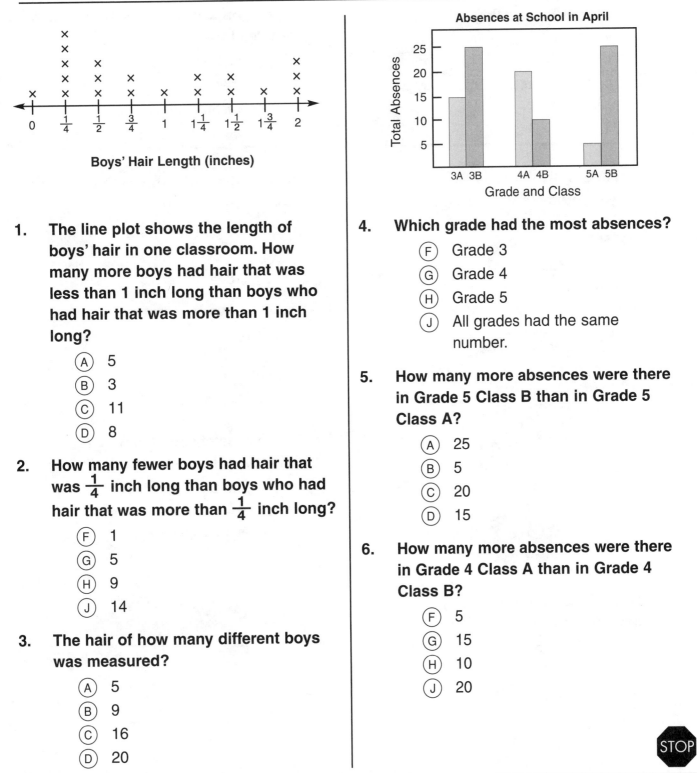

Boys' Hair Length (inches)

Absences at School in April

Grade and Class

1. The line plot shows the length of boys' hair in one classroom. How many more boys had hair that was less than 1 inch long than boys who had hair that was more than 1 inch long?
   - Ⓐ 5
   - Ⓑ 3
   - Ⓒ 11
   - Ⓓ 8

2. How many fewer boys had hair that was $\frac{1}{4}$ inch long than boys who had hair that was more than $\frac{1}{4}$ inch long?
   - Ⓕ 1
   - Ⓖ 5
   - Ⓗ 9
   - Ⓙ 14

3. The hair of how many different boys was measured?
   - Ⓐ 5
   - Ⓑ 9
   - Ⓒ 16
   - Ⓓ 20

4. Which grade had the most absences?
   - Ⓕ Grade 3
   - Ⓖ Grade 4
   - Ⓗ Grade 5
   - Ⓙ All grades had the same number.

5. How many more absences were there in Grade 5 Class B than in Grade 5 Class A?
   - Ⓐ 25
   - Ⓑ 5
   - Ⓒ 20
   - Ⓓ 15

6. How many more absences were there in Grade 4 Class A than in Grade 4 Class B?
   - Ⓕ 5
   - Ⓖ 15
   - Ⓗ 10
   - Ⓙ 20

STOP

Name _____ Date_____

MATH: APPLICATIONS
SAMPLE TEST

Directions: Read and work each problem. Find the correct answer. Mark the space for your choice.

Examples

A. A cereal box is shaped like a—
- (A) pyramid.
- (B) sphere.
- (C) rectangular prism.
- (D) cone.

B. A polygon with three sides and three vertices is a—
- (F) square.
- (G) triangle.
- (H) rectangular prism.
- (J) octagon.

1. **Which of these shapes is symmetrical?**

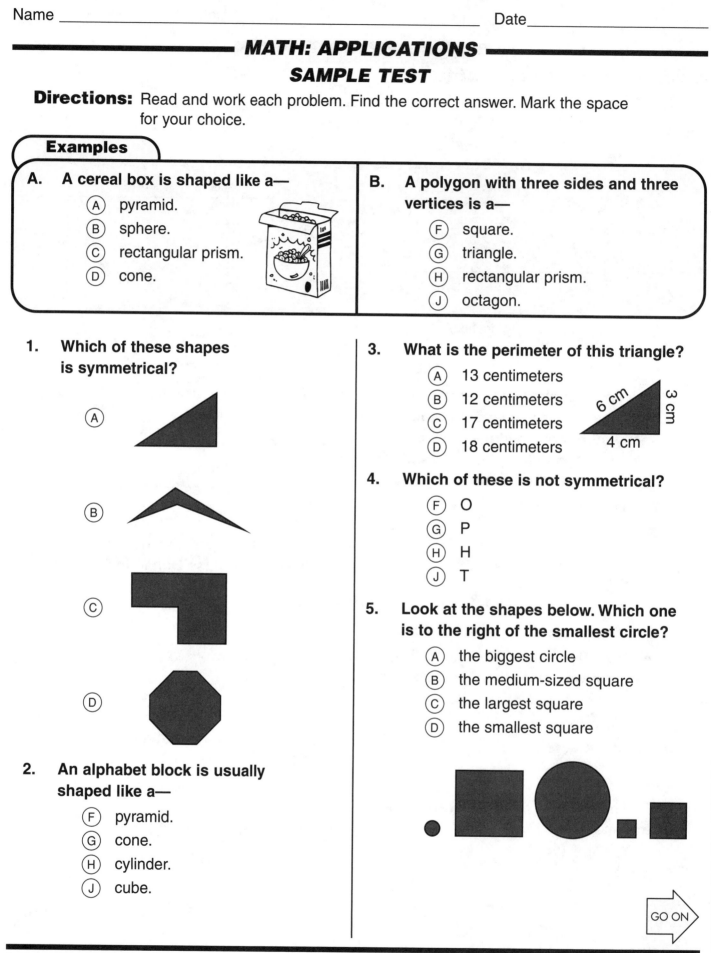

- (A)
- (B)
- (C)
- (D)

2. **An alphabet block is usually shaped like a—**
- (F) pyramid.
- (G) cone.
- (H) cylinder.
- (J) cube.

3. **What is the perimeter of this triangle?**
- (A) 13 centimeters
- (B) 12 centimeters
- (C) 17 centimeters
- (D) 18 centimeters

6 cm 3 cm 4 cm

4. **Which of these is not symmetrical?**
- (F) O
- (G) P
- (H) H
- (J) T

5. **Look at the shapes below. Which one is to the right of the smallest circle?**
- (A) the biggest circle
- (B) the medium-sized square
- (C) the largest square
- (D) the smallest square

GO ON

MATH: APPLICATIONS
SAMPLE TEST (cont.)

Read and work each problem. Find the correct answer. Mark the space for your choice.

6. Look at the calendar page. What is the date of the second Monday of the month?

March						
Sunday	Monday	Tuesday	Wednesday	Thursday	Friday	Saturday
	1	2	3	4	5	6
7	8	9	10	11	12	13
14	15	16	17	18	19	20
21	22	23	24	25	26	27
28	29	30	31			

- (F) March 1
- (G) March 7
- (H) March 8
- (J) March 2

7. Rita left dance class at 3:30. She arrived home at 4:17. How long did it take Rita to get home?

- (A) 1 hour, 17 minutes
- (B) 47 minutes
- (C) 37 minutes
- (D) 13 minutes

8. How long is the paperclip?

- (F) 3 inches
- (G) 5 inches
- (H) 3 centimeters
- (J) 2 centimeters

9. Keisha measured the length of a room at 8 feet. How many inches long is the room?

- (A) 16 inches
- (B) 24 inches
- (C) 96 inches
- (D) 106 inches

10. In the morning, the temperature was 56° F. By noon, the temperature had risen by 9° F. How warm was it at noon?

- (F) 60° F
- (G) 64° F
- (H) 65° F
- (J) 70° F

GO ON

MATH: APPLICATIONS
SAMPLE TEST (cont.)

Read and work each problem. Find the correct answer. Mark the space for your choice.

11. Which combination of coins makes $0.40?

(A) 1 nickel, 1 dime, 1 half-dollar
(B) 2 dimes, 1 nickel, 5 pennies
(C) 3 dimes, 1 nickel, 1 penny
(D) 1 nickel, 1 dime, 1 quarter

12. How many bicycles and cars would you need to have a total of 26 wheels?

(F) 6 cars and 1 bicycle
(G) 5 cars and 2 bicycles
(H) 4 cars and 3 bicycles
(J) 2 cars and 7 bicycles

13. Kelton is 9 centimeters shorter than Stewart. If Stewart is 122 centimeters tall, Kelton is—

(A) 112 centimeters tall.
(B) 111 centimeters tall.
(C) 113 centimeters tall.
(D) 103 centimeters tall.

14. Which of these numbers would round to 300?

(F) 226
(G) 249
(H) 252
(J) 239

15. Cody played in 3 basketball games. In the first game, he scored 17 points. In the second game, he scored 22 points. In the third game, he scored twice as many points as in his first game. His points for the third game totaled—

(A) 44 points.
(B) 36 points.
(C) 34 points.
(D) 42 points.

16. Andre bought 12 game tokens at 3:00. At 6:00, he bought 24 more tokens. If each token cost $0.20, how much did he spend on tokens in all?

(F) $2.40
(G) $4.80
(H) $7.20
(J) $6.80

GO ON

MATH: APPLICATIONS
SAMPLE TEST (cont.)

Read and work each problem. Find the correct answer. Mark the space for your choice.

Look at the price information. Use it to answer questions 17–20.

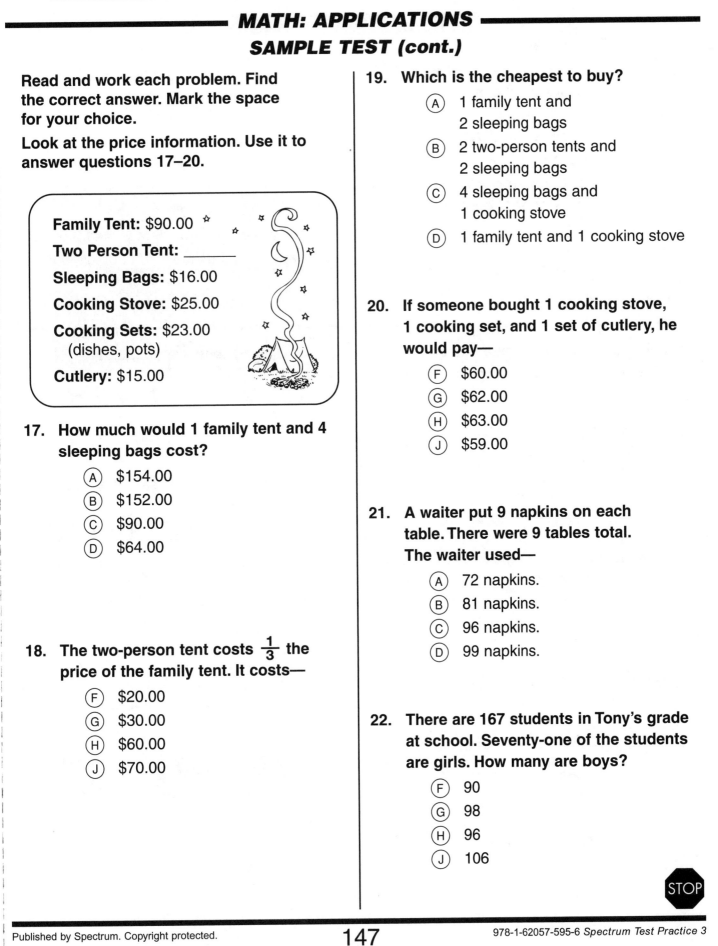

Family Tent: $90.00

Two Person Tent: _____

Sleeping Bags: $16.00

Cooking Stove: $25.00

Cooking Sets: $23.00
(dishes, pots)

Cutlery: $15.00

17. How much would 1 family tent and 4 sleeping bags cost?

- (A) $154.00
- (B) $152.00
- (C) $90.00
- (D) $64.00

18. The two-person tent costs $\frac{1}{3}$ the price of the family tent. It costs—

- (F) $20.00
- (G) $30.00
- (H) $60.00
- (J) $70.00

19. Which is the cheapest to buy?

- (A) 1 family tent and 2 sleeping bags
- (B) 2 two-person tents and 2 sleeping bags
- (C) 4 sleeping bags and 1 cooking stove
- (D) 1 family tent and 1 cooking stove

20. If someone bought 1 cooking stove, 1 cooking set, and 1 set of cutlery, he would pay—

- (F) $60.00
- (G) $62.00
- (H) $63.00
- (J) $59.00

21. A waiter put 9 napkins on each table. There were 9 tables total. The waiter used—

- (A) 72 napkins.
- (B) 81 napkins.
- (C) 96 napkins.
- (D) 99 napkins.

22. There are 167 students in Tony's grade at school. Seventy-one of the students are girls. How many are boys?

- (F) 90
- (G) 98
- (H) 96
- (J) 106

STOP

MATH PRACTICE TEST

● **Part 1: Concepts**

Directions: Read and work each problem. Find the correct answer. Mark the space for your choice.

Examples

A. You bought 27 trading cards. You gave away 19 of them. How can you find the number of cards that are left?

- (A) add
- (B) subtract
- (C) multiply
- (D) divide

B. What is another name for 2,453?

- (F) 2 thousands, 4 hundreds, 3 tens, and 5 ones
- (G) 2 hundreds, 5 tens, and 3 ones
- (H) 2 thousands, 4 hundreds, 5 tens, and 3 ones
- (J) 4 hundreds, 5 tens, and 3 ones

---

1. You are number 11 in a line of 30 people. How many people are ahead of you?

- (A) 19
- (B) 11
- (C) 10
- (D) 20

2. What is another name for 4 hundreds, 2 tens, and 8 ones?

- (F) 284
- (G) 482
- (H) 428
- (J) 824

3. Which number is less than 807?

- (A) 806
- (B) 808
- (C) 809
- (D) 810

4. How many tens are in 1,525?

- (F) 5
- (G) 6
- (H) 2
- (J) 1

5. What number is represented by the chart?

Hundreds	Tens	Ones
I I I I I	I I I	I I I I I I I

- (A) 737
- (B) 573
- (C) 436
- (D) 537

6. Look at the number pattern in the box. Find the number that is missing.

11	22	___	44	55

- (F) 33
- (G) 23
- (H) 66
- (J) 42

GO ON

MATH PRACTICE TEST
Part 1: Concepts (cont.)

7. The pattern is apple, pear, banana, orange. Which is the missing piece of fruit in the third row?

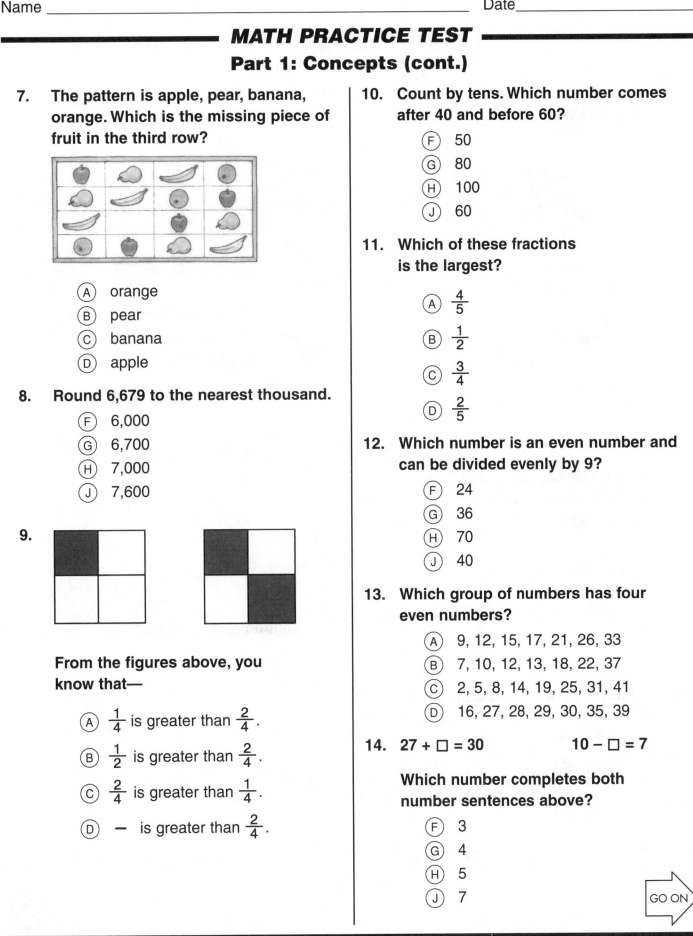

- (A) orange
- (B) pear
- (C) banana
- (D) apple

8. Round 6,679 to the nearest thousand.

- (F) 6,000
- (G) 6,700
- (H) 7,000
- (J) 7,600

9.

From the figures above, you know that—

- (A) $\frac{1}{4}$ is greater than $\frac{2}{4}$.
- (B) $\frac{1}{2}$ is greater than $\frac{2}{4}$.
- (C) $\frac{2}{4}$ is greater than $\frac{1}{4}$.
- (D) — is greater than $\frac{2}{4}$.

10. Count by tens. Which number comes after 40 and before 60?

- (F) 50
- (G) 80
- (H) 100
- (J) 60

11. Which of these fractions is the largest?

- (A) $\frac{4}{5}$
- (B) $\frac{1}{2}$
- (C) $\frac{3}{4}$
- (D) $\frac{2}{5}$

12. Which number is an even number and can be divided evenly by 9?

- (F) 24
- (G) 36
- (H) 70
- (J) 40

13. Which group of numbers has four even numbers?

- (A) 9, 12, 15, 17, 21, 26, 33
- (B) 7, 10, 12, 13, 18, 22, 37
- (C) 2, 5, 8, 14, 19, 25, 31, 41
- (D) 16, 27, 28, 29, 30, 35, 39

14. $27 + \square = 30$ $10 - \square = 7$

Which number completes both number sentences above?

- (F) 3
- (G) 4
- (H) 5
- (J) 7

GO ON

MATH PRACTICE TEST
Part 1: Concepts (cont.)

15. Which number sentence shows the total number of beans?

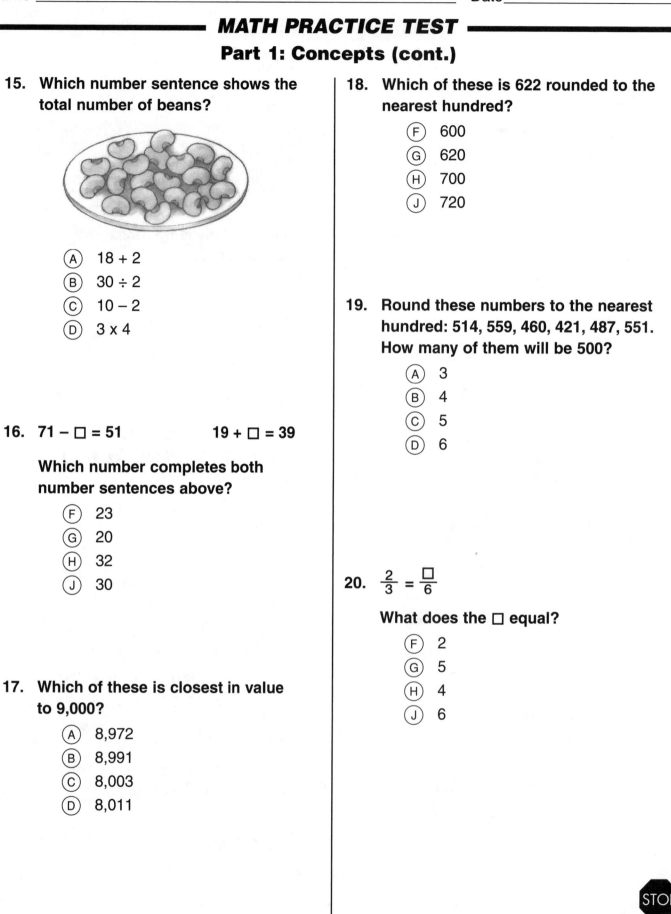

- (A) 18 + 2
- (B) 30 ÷ 2
- (C) 10 − 2
- (D) 3 x 4

16. 71 − □ = 51   19 + □ = 39

Which number completes both number sentences above?

- (F) 23
- (G) 20
- (H) 32
- (J) 30

17. Which of these is closest in value to 9,000?

- (A) 8,972
- (B) 8,991
- (C) 8,003
- (D) 8,011

18. Which of these is 622 rounded to the nearest hundred?

- (F) 600
- (G) 620
- (H) 700
- (J) 720

19. Round these numbers to the nearest hundred: 514, 559, 460, 421, 487, 551. How many of them will be 500?

- (A) 3
- (B) 4
- (C) 5
- (D) 6

20. $\frac{2}{3} = \frac{\square}{6}$

What does the □ equal?

- (F) 2
- (G) 5
- (H) 4
- (J) 6

STOP

Name _____ Date _____

● Part 2: Computation

Directions: Mark the space for the correct answer to each problem. Choose "None of these" if the right answer is not given.

Examples

A. 345
     + 34

- Ⓐ 311
- Ⓑ 379
- Ⓒ 369
- Ⓓ None of these

B. 98 − 69 =

- Ⓕ 39
- Ⓖ 29
- Ⓗ 167
- Ⓙ None of these

---

1. 321
     − 75

- Ⓐ 246
- Ⓑ 396
- Ⓒ 386
- Ⓓ None of these

2. $\frac{4}{7} - \frac{3}{7} =$

- Ⓕ $\frac{2}{7}$
- Ⓖ $\frac{3}{7}$
- Ⓗ $\frac{1}{7}$
- Ⓙ None of these

3. $\frac{7}{10} - \frac{3}{10} =$

- Ⓐ $\frac{5}{10}$
- Ⓑ $\frac{4}{10}$
- Ⓒ $\frac{3}{10}$
- Ⓓ None of these

4. 25 + 25 + 6 =

- Ⓕ 51
- Ⓖ 56
- Ⓗ 61
- Ⓙ None of these

5. 3,000
     − 1,350

- Ⓐ 1,650
- Ⓑ 4,350
- Ⓒ 4,400
- Ⓓ None of these

6. 2.99
     − 1.15

- Ⓕ 4.16
- Ⓖ 4.14
- Ⓗ 4.15
- Ⓙ None of these

7. 622
     + 222

- Ⓐ 844
- Ⓑ 400
- Ⓒ 422
- Ⓓ None of these

8. 15 − 9 =

- Ⓕ 5
- Ⓖ 6
- Ⓗ 7
- Ⓙ None of these

9. 35 + 21 + 9 =

- Ⓐ 55
- Ⓑ 60
- Ⓒ 65
- Ⓓ None of these

10. $7.19 − $2.20 =

- Ⓕ $9.39
- Ⓖ $9.99
- Ⓗ $4.99
- Ⓙ None of these

GO ON ▷

MATH PRACTICE TEST
Part 2: Computation (cont.)

Mark the space for the correct answer to each problem. Choose "None of these" if the right answer is not given.

11.   551
+ 17

- Ⓐ 568
- Ⓑ 578
- Ⓒ 534
- Ⓓ None of these

12.   5,670
+ 128

- Ⓕ 5,799
- Ⓖ 5,797
- Ⓗ 5,796
- Ⓙ None of these

13. $\frac{4}{5} - \frac{1}{5} =$

- Ⓐ $\frac{3}{10}$
- Ⓑ $\frac{3}{5}$
- Ⓒ $\frac{1}{5}$
- Ⓓ None of these

14. $5\overline{)200}$

- Ⓕ 50
- Ⓖ 40
- Ⓗ 30
- Ⓙ None of these

15.   4,009
− 35

- Ⓐ 3,994
- Ⓑ 4,044
- Ⓒ 3,974
- Ⓓ None of these

16.   0.98
− 0.29

- Ⓕ 1.27
- Ⓖ 0.79
- Ⓗ 0.69
- Ⓙ None of these

17.   77
x 6

- Ⓐ 472
- Ⓑ 460
- Ⓒ 464
- Ⓓ None of these

18. $6\overline{)62}$

- Ⓕ 10 R1
- Ⓖ 10
- Ⓗ 10 R2
- Ⓙ None of these

19. $1\frac{3}{4} - \frac{1}{4} =$

- Ⓐ $1\frac{2}{4}$
- Ⓑ $1\frac{3}{4}$
- Ⓒ $1\frac{5}{4}$
- Ⓓ None of these

20. $\$4.25 - \$1.15 =$

- Ⓕ $4.40
- Ⓖ $5.40
- Ⓗ $3.10
- Ⓙ None of these

STOP

Name _____ Date _____

MATH PRACTICE TEST

● Part 3: Applications

Directions: Read and work each problem. Find the correct answer. Mark the space for your choice.

Examples

A. A piece of pizza is shaped most like a—

- (A) triangle.
- (B) sphere.
- (C) circle.
- (D) octagon.

B. A lamp that is 23 inches tall is—

- (F) less than 2 feet tall.
- (G) more than 2 feet tall.
- (H) less than 1 foot tall.
- (J) equal to 2 feet in height.

---

1. Taina had a rectangle made out of paper. She drew a line down the middle of the rectangle and then she drew a line diagonal through the rectangle. She then had 4 shapes drawn. What is one shape she made?

- (A) square
- (B) circle
- (C) triangle
- (D) oval

2. $\frac{2}{3} \square \frac{3}{2}$

Choose the correct symbol to go in the box.

- (F) <
- (G) >
- (H) =
- (J) Not enough information

3. Which of these is symmetrical?

- (A) U
- (B) L
- (C) K
- (D) Q

Look at the graph. Use it to answer numbers 4–5.

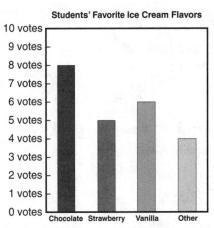

Students' Favorite Ice Cream Flavors

4. How many students named vanilla as their favorite?

- (F) 2
- (G) 6
- (H) 8
- (J) Not enough information

5. How many more students voted for chocolate ice cream than for strawberry?

- (A) 3
- (B) 8
- (C) 13
- (D) Not enough information

GO ON

Name _____ Date _____

Read and work each problem. Find the correct answer. Mark the space for your choice.

6. Look at the clock. How long will it take the minute hand to reach the 6?

- (F) 3 minutes
- (G) 5 minutes
- (H) 12 minutes
- (J) 15 minutes

7. What unit of weight would be best to weigh a young child?
- (A) ounces
- (B) pints
- (C) pounds
- (D) tons

Look at the calendar page. Use it to answer numbers 8–11.

APRIL						
Sunday	Monday	Tuesday	Wednesday	Thursday	Friday	Saturday
				1	2	3
4	5	6	7	8	9	10
11	12	13	14	15	16	17
18	19	20	21	22	23	24
25	26	27	28	29	30	

8. Mr. and Mrs. Akers are going to build a deck. It will take 2 weeks to finish. They plan to start on April 7. What date will they finish?
- (F) April 24
- (G) April 21
- (H) April 14
- (J) April 23

9. Mrs. Akers is going to plant flowers around the new deck. She plans to buy the flowers on April 24 and be done in 2 days. What are the days of the week on which she will be planting flowers?
- (A) Friday and Saturday
- (B) Saturday and Sunday
- (C) Sunday and Monday
- (D) Not enough information

10. Mr. and Mrs. Akers are leaving on a trip on Monday, April 26. If they are returning the following Saturday, on what date will they return?
- (F) April 30
- (G) April 27
- (H) May 1
- (J) May 2

11. Mr. Simms has 4 boxes. In each box are 16 candles. Mr. Simms wants to use all of the candles and put an equal number on each of 8 tables. How many candles will be on each table?
- (A) 64 candles
- (B) 8 candles
- (C) 32 candles
- (D) 56 candles

READING: VOCABULARY
Lesson 1: Synonyms
• Page 7
  A. D
  B. H
  1. B
  2. F
  3. D
  4. G
  5. C
  6. G

Lesson 2: Vocabulary Skills
• Page 8
  A. D
  B. G
  1. A
  2. J
  3. A
  4. H
  5. B
  6. J
  7. C
  8. J

Lesson 3: Antonyms
• Page 9
  A. B
  B. J
  1. D
  2. H
  3. B
  4. G
  5. B
  6. F
  7. D
  8. F

Lesson 4: Multi-Meaning Words
• Page 10
  A. C
  B. H
  1. C
  2. J
  3. C
  4. G
  5. C
  6. G

Lesson 5: Words in Context
• Page 11
  A. C
  B. H
  1. D
  2. G
  3. C
  4. G
  5. A
  6. H

Lesson 6: Prefixes
• Page 12
  A. B
  B. G
  1. B
  2. F
  3. D
  4. H
  5. B
  6. F

Lesson 7: Suffixes
• Page 13
  A. C

  B. J
  1. A
  2. G
  3. D
  4. H
  5. B
  6. J

Lesson 8: Comparatives and Superlatives
• Page 14
  A. C
  B. G
  1. A
  2. G
  3. D
  4. G
  5. A
  6. H

Lesson 9: Root Words
• Page 15
  A. D
  B. G
  1. C
  2. J
  3. C
  4. G
  5. A
  6. G

Lesson 10: Words About Time and Space
• Page 16
  A. C
  B. F
  1. C
  2. J
  3. A
  4. H

Lesson 11: Word Relationships
• Page 17
  1. B
  2. H
  3. C
  4. F
  5. C
  6. G
  7. C

Sample Test
• Pages 18–19
  A. D
  B. F
  1. D
  2. H
  3. A
  4. G
  5. D
  6. G
  7. A
  8. G
  9. A
  10. J
  11. B
  12. J
  13. B
  14. F
  15. C
  16. J
  17. A

READING: READING COMPREHENSION
Lesson 12: Main Idea
• Page 20
  A. C
  1. C
  2. G
  3. C

Lesson 13: Recalling Details
• Page 21
  A. C
  1. C
  2. J
  3. C

Lesson 14: Inferencing
• Page 22
  A. C
  1. D
  2. J
  3. A
  4. J

Lesson 15: Fact and Opinion
• Page 23
  A. C
  1. D
  2. F
  3. C
  4. H

Lesson 16: Story Elements
• Page 24
  A. A
  1. B
  2. H
  3. D

Lesson 17: Fiction
• Page 25
  A. B
  1. C
  2. H
  3. D
  4. G

Lesson 18: Fiction
• Pages 26–27
  A. C
  1. C
  2. H
  3. A
  4. H
  5. D
  6. G
  7. B

Lesson 19: Fiction
• Pages 28–29
  A. B
  1. D
  2. G
  3. D
  4. G
  5. B
  6. F
  7. B
  8. F

Lesson 20: Reading Literature
• Pages 30–31
  1. A
  2. H
  3. B
  4. H

5. A
6. H
7. B
8. J
9. D
10. F

Lesson 21: Nonfiction
• Page 32
A. B
1. C
2. H
3. B
4. G

Lesson 22: Nonfiction
• Page 33
A. C
1. C
2. G
3. B

Lesson 23: Nonfiction
• Pages 34–35
A. B
1. A
2. G
3. B
4. J
5. D
6. G
7. C
8. G

Lesson 24: Reading Informational Text
• Pages 36–37
1. D
2. H
3. A
4. J
5. A
6. G
7. B
8. J

Sample Test
• Pages 38–41
A. B
1. B
2. G
3. B
4. G
5. C
6. F
7. D
8. H
B. C
9. A
10. H
11. D
12. F
13. A
14. G
15. C

READING PRACTICE TEST
Part 1: Vocabulary
• Pages 42–44
A. B
B. F
1. C
2. F
3. D

4. H
5. C
6. F
7. D
8. F
9. B
10. F
11. B
12. J
13. C
14. G
15. D
16. H
17. A
18. G
19. C
20. J
21. C
22. G
23. A
24. H
25. D

Part 2: Reading Comprehension
• Pages 45–51
A. C
1. B
2. F
3. C
4. H
5. B
6. H
7. B
8. H
9. D
10. G
11. C
12. H
13. C
14. J
15. C
16. F
17. B
18. F
19. D
20. J
21. C
22. G
23. B

LANGUAGE: LANGUAGE MECHANICS
Lesson 1: Capitalization
• Page 52
A. D
B. H
1. A
2. H
3. C
4. G
5. A

Lesson 2: Punctuation
• Page 53
A. D
B. F
1. C
2. F
3. B
4. H
5. C

Lesson 3: Capitalization and Punctuation
• Page 54
A. D
B. H
1. C
2. H
3. C
4. H
5. A

Lesson 4: Using Commas
• Page 55
A. C
B. F
1. D
2. G
3. C
4. H
5. B
6. F

Lesson 5: Possessives
• Page 56
A. A
B. J
1. C
2. G
3. A
4. G
5. B
6. F

Sample Test
• Pages 57–59
A. C
B. G
1. D
2. H
3. A
4. H
5. C
6. J
7. A
8. H
9. B
10. F
11. A
12. G
13. D
14. J
15. C
16. H
17. D
18. G
19. A
20. J
21. B
22. H
23. D

LANGUAGE: LANGUAGE EXPRESSION
Lesson 6: Nouns and Pronouns
• Pages 60–61
A. C
B. G
1. D
2. H
3. B
4. H
5. B

6. J
C. A
D. G
7. B
8. J
9. C
10. G
11. A
12. F

Lesson 7: Verbs
• Page 62
A. B
B. F
1. B
2. J
3. B
4. F
5. B
6. H

Lesson 8: Adjectives
• Page 63
A. C
B. G
1. D
2. F
3. C
4. G
5. B
6. H

Lesson 9: Sentences
• Pages 64–66
A. A
B. J
1. A
2. H
3. D
4. F
5. A
6. G
7. C
8. F
9. C
10. F
11. C
12. G
13. A
14. J

Lesson 10: Paragraphs
• Pages 67–69
A. A
1. C
2. G
3. A
4. F
5. A
6. G
7. A
8. F
9. C
10. J
11. C

Sample Test
• Pages 70–76
A. A
B. G
1. D
2. H
3. B

4. H
5. B
6. J
7. B
8. F
9. B
10. J
11. A
12. H
13. A
14. H
15. C
16. J
17. D
18. F
19. A
20. H
21. B
22. G
23. B
24. J
25. A
26. J
27. B
28. G
29. C
30. G
31. C
32. F
33. D
34. G
35. C
36. J
37. D
38. F
39. C
40. J
41. A
42. H
43. B

LANGUAGE: SPELLING
Lesson 11: Spelling
• Pages 77–78
A. B
B. J
1. B
2. J
3. B
4. H
5. A
6. G
7. A
8. G
9. B
10. G
11. D
12. H
13. D
14. G
15. A
16. H
17. A
18. G
19. D
20. G

Lesson 12: Spelling Regular and Irregular Plurals
• Page 79

A. C
B. J
1. B
2. F
3. B
4. H
5. A
6. J

Sample Test
• Pages 80–81
A. A
B. H
1. C
2. F
3. B
4. J
5. D
6. F
7. C
8. G
9. D
10. H
11. A
12. F
13. D
14. H
15. D
16. H
17. A
18. F
19. B
20. J
21. B
22. J

LANGUAGE: STUDY SKILLS
Lesson 13: Study Skills
• Pages 82–84
A. D
B. J
1. C
2. F
3. D
4. H
5. A
6. J
7. D
8. H
9. C
10. J
11. C
12. G
13. C
14. J
15. C
16. H
17. C
18. G
19. B
20. F

Sample Test
• Pages 85–86
A. D
B. G
1. D
2. J
3. D
4. H
5. B

6. G
7. A
8. G
9. A
10. H
11. B
12. G
13. D
14. F

LANGUAGE PRACTICE TEST
Part 1: Language Mechanics
• Pages 89–91
A. B
B. F
1. C
2. F
3. C
4. J
5. A
6. F
7. B
8. J
9. A
10. H
11. D
12. H
13. D
14. G
15. A
16. G
17. D
18. G
19. A
20. J
21. C
22. H

Part 2: Language Expression
• Pages 92–95
A. C
B. H
1. A
2. H
3. B
4. J
5. B
6. F
7. A
8. H
9. A
10. H
11. B
12. F
13. B
14. G
15. B
16. J
17. C
18. H
19. D
20. F
21. A
22. B
23. B
24. F
25. C
26. J
27. A

Part 3: Spelling
• Pages 96–97
A. B
B. F
1. C
2. J
3. A
4. G
5. B
6. H
7. D
8. F
9. B
10. G
11. B
12. H
13. D
14. H
15. A
16. F
17. A
18. G
19. D
20. F
21. D
22. H

Part 4: Study Skills
• Pages 98–99
A. C
B. F
1. A
2. H
3. B
4. J
5. C
6. G
7. C
8. F
9. D
10. H
11. B
12. H
13. A
14. J
15. A
16. J

MATH: CONCEPTS
Lesson 1: Numeration
• Pages 100–102
A. C
B. J
1. C
2. G
3. B
4. F
5. B
6. J
7. C
8. H
9. D
10. G
11. D
12. G
13. D
14. G
15. A
16. J
17. C

18. G
Lesson 2: Number Concepts
• Pages 103–104
A. A
B. H
1. C
2. G
3. D
4. F
5. D
6. J
7. C
8. F
9. B
10. G
11. B
12. G

Lesson 3: Properties
• Pages 105–106
A. C
B. H
1. C
2. H
3. B
4. G
5. D
6. G
7. B
8. G
9. D
10. G
11. D

Lesson 4: Properties of Operations
• Page 107
A. A
B. H
1. A
2. J
3. B
4. J

Lesson 5: Multiplication and Division
• Pages 108–110
A. C
B. F
1. A
2. G
3. B
4. J
5. D
6. J
7. A
8. F
9. C
10. J
11. A
12. H
13. B
14. J
15. A
16. H
17. D
18. H
19. D
20. F
21. A
22. G

Lesson 6: Understanding Fractions
• Pages 111–112
- A. C
- B. H
- 1. C
- 2. G
- 3. B
- 4. H
- 5. B
- 6. G
- 7. A
- 8. H
- 9. D
- 10. J
- 11. B
- 12. G
- 13. A
- 14. F

Lesson 7: Comparing Fractions
• Pages 113–114
- A. D
- B. F
- 1. C
- 2. F
- 3. C
- 4. J
- 5. B
- 6. F
- 7. C
- 8. G
- 9. D
- 10. F
- 11. C
- 12. F
- 13. D
- 14. F

Sample Test
• Pages 115–117
- A. B
- B. J
- 1. C
- 2. G
- 3. A
- 4. J
- 5. B
- 6. J
- 7. D
- 8. G
- 9. C
- 10. H
- 11. D
- 12. H
- 13. A
- 14. H
- 15. D
- 16. H
- 17. B
- 18. J
- 19. A
- 20. F

MATH: COMPUTATION
Lesson 8: Addition
• Pages 118–119
- A. C
- B. J
- 1. C
- 2. G

- 3. C
- 4. J
- 5. A
- 6. G
- 7. D
- 8. H
- 9. C
- 10. J
- 11. B
- 12. H
- 13. D
- 14. F
- 15. D
- 16. G
- 17. C
- 18. J

Lesson 9: Subtraction
• Pages 120–121
- A. B
- B. F
- 1. C
- 2. J
- 3. B
- 4. J
- 5. A
- 6. H
- 7. B
- 8. H
- 9. A
- 10. J
- 11. C
- 12. H
- 13. C
- 14. G
- 15. D
- 16. G
- 17. C
- 18. G

Lesson 10: Multiplication and Division
• Pages 122–123
- A. C
- B. H
- 1. A
- 2. G
- 3. C
- 4. H
- 5. D
- 6. G
- 7. A
- 8. H
- 9. C
- 10. F
- 11. B
- 12. H
- 13. B
- 14. F
- 15. D
- 16. J
- 17. B
- 18. H

Lesson 11: Rounding Whole Numbers
• Page 124
- A. C
- 1. A
- 2. J
- 3. B

- 4. J
- 5. C
- 6. J
- 7. B
- 8. J

Sample Test
• Pages 125–127
- A. C
- B. G
- 1. C
- 2. F
- 3. A
- 4. H
- 5. C
- 6. J
- 7. D
- 8. J
- 9. B
- 10. F
- 11. B
- 12. H
- 13. C
- 14. H
- 15. A
- 16. F
- 17. C
- 18. G
- 19. B
- 20. G
- 21. C
- 22. J
- 23. C
- 24. F
- 25. C
- 26. H
- 27. A
- 28. G
- 29. B
- 30. G
- 31. B
- 32. H
- 33. C
- 34. J

MATH: APPLICATIONS
Lesson 12: Geometry
• Pages 128–131
- A. B
- 1. C
- 2. G
- 3. C
- 4. H
- 5. B
- 6. J
- 7. C
- 8. H
- 9. A
- 10. J
- 11. C
- 12. F
- 13. C
- 14. G
- 15. A
- 16. G
- 17. C
- 18. J

Lesson 13: Shapes and Their Attributes
• Page 132
A. C
B. F
1. B
2. J
3. C
4. H
5. A

Lesson 14: Measurement
• Pages 133–136
A. C
1. A
2. J
3. C
4. H
5. C
6. G
7. C
8. H
9. B
10. F
11. D
12. H
13. B
14. G
15. D
16. H
17. D
18. J
19. D
20. F
21. B

Lesson 15: Finding Area
• Page 137
A. D
B. G
1. C
2. J
3. C
4. G
5. B
6. J

Lesson 16: Mass and Liquid Volume
• Page 138
A. A
1. C
2. G
3. A
4. H
5. C
6. H

Lesson 17: Problem-Solving
• Pages 139–142
A. B
1. C
2. G
3. D
4. G
5. D
6. H
7. D
8. H
9. B
10. H
11. B

12. H
13. A
14. G
15. B
16. J
17. C
18. J
19. B
20. G
21. D
22. J

Lesson 18: Interpret Data
• Page 143
1. B
2. H
3. D
4. F
5. C
6. H

Sample Test
• Pages 144–147
A. C
B. G
1. D
2. J
3. A
4. G
5. C
6. H
7. B
8. H
9. C
10. H
11. D
12. F
13. C
14. H
15. C
16. H
17. A
18. G
19. B
20. H
21. B
22. H

MATH PRACTICE TEST
Part 1: Concepts
• Pages 148–150
A. B
B. H
1. C
2. H
3. A
4. H
5. D
6. F
7. A
8. H
9. C
10. F
11. A
12. G
13. B
14. F
15. A
16. G
17. B
18. F

19. A
20. H
Part 2: Computation
• Pages 151–152
A. B
B. G
1. A
2. H
3. B
4. G
5. A
6. J
7. A
8. G
9. C
10. H
11. A
12. J
13. B
14. G
15. C
16. H
17. D
18. H
19. A
20. H

Part 3: Applications
• Pages 153–154
A. A
B. F
1. C
2. F
3. A
4. G
5. A
6. J
7. C
8. G
9. C
10. H
11. B